P9-BAU-944

PRENTICE HALL

PRE-ALGEBRA

Practice Workbook

Prentice
Hall

Needham, Massachusetts
Upper Saddle River, New Jersey
Glenview, Illinois

Copyright © 2001 by Prentice-Hall, Inc., Upper Saddle River, New Jersey 07458.
All rights reserved. Printed in the United States of America. This publication is
protected by Copyright and permission should be obtained from the publisher prior
to any prohibited reproduction, storage in a retrieval system, or transmission in any
form or by any means, electronic, mechanical, photocopying, recording, or likewise.
Student worksheets and tests may be reproduced for classroom use, the number not
to exceed the number of students in each class. For information regarding
permission(s), write to: Rights and Permissions Department.

ISBN 0-13-050475-0

10   05 04 03 02

Table of Contents

Table of Contents (continued)

Practice 1-1 *Variables and Expressions*

Write an expression for each quantity.

1. the value in cents of 5 quarters _____

2. the value in cents of *q* quarters _____

3. the number of months in 7 years _____

4. the number of months in *y* years _____

5. the number of gallons in 21 quarts _____

6. the number of gallons in *q* quarts _____

Write a variable expression for each word phrase.

7. 9 less than *k*

_____

8. *m* divided by 6

_____

9. twice *x*

_____

10. 4 more than twice *x*

_____

11. the sum of eighteen and *b*

_____

12. three times the quantity 2 plus *a*

_____

Tell whether each expression is a numerical expression or a variable expression. For a variable expression, name the variable.

13. $4d$ _____

14. $74 + 8$ _____

15. $\frac{4(9)}{6}$ _____

16. $14 - p$ _____

17. $5k - 9$ _____

18. $3 + 3 + 3 + 3$ _____

19. $19 + 3(12)$ _____

20. $25 - 9 + x$ _____

The room temperature is *c* degrees centigrade. Write a word phrase for each expression.

21. $c + 15$

_____

22. $c - 7$

_____

Practice 1-2 *The Order of Operations*

Simplify each expression.

1. $3 + 15 - 5 \cdot 2$ _____

2. $5 \cdot 6 + 2 \cdot 4$ _____

3. $48 \div 8 - 1$ _____

4. $68 - 12 \div 2 \div 3$ _____

5. $6(2 + 7)$ _____

6. $25 - (6 \cdot 4)$ _____

7. $3[9 - (6 - 3)] - 10$ _____

8. $60 \div (3 + 12)$ _____

9. $4 - 2 + 6 \cdot 2$ _____

10. $18 \div (5 - 2)$ _____

11. $\frac{16 + 24}{30 - 22}$ _____

12. $2[4(9 - 7) + 1]$ _____

13. $(8 \div 8 + 2 + 11) \div 2$ _____

14. $9 + 3 \cdot 4$ _____

15. $18 \div 3 \cdot 5 - 4$ _____

16. $10 + 28 \div 14 - 5$ _____

Insert grouping symbols to make each number sentence true.

17. $3 + 5 \cdot 8 = 64$

18. $4 \cdot 6 - 2 + 7 = 23$

19. $10 \div 3 + 2 \cdot 4 = 8$

20. $3 + 6 \cdot 2 = 18$

A city park has two walkways with a grassy area in the center, as shown in the diagram.

21. Write an expression for the area of the sidewalks, using subtraction.

_____

22. Write an expression for the area of the sidewalks, using addition.

_____

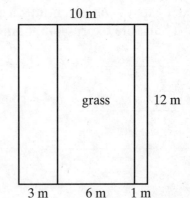

Compare. Use >, <, or = to complete statement.

23. $(24 - 8) \div 4 \;\boxed{}\; 24 - 8 \div 4$

24. $3 \cdot (4 - 2) \cdot 5 \;\boxed{}\; 3 \cdot 4 - 2 \cdot 5$

25. $(22 + 8) \div 2 \;\boxed{}\; 22 + 8 \div 2$

26. $20 \div 2 + 8 \cdot 2 \;\boxed{}\; 20 \div (2 + 8) \cdot 2$

27. $11 \cdot 4 - 2 \;\boxed{}\; 11 \cdot (4 - 2)$

28. $(7 \cdot 3) - (4 \cdot 2) \;\boxed{}\; 7 \cdot 3 - 4 \cdot 2$

Practice 1-3 Evaluating Expressions

Evaluate each expression.

1. xy, for $x = 3$ and $y = 5$ _____

2. $24 - p \cdot 5$, for $p = 4$ _____

3. $5a + b$, for $a = 6$ and $b = 3$ _____

4. $6x$, for $x = 3$ _____

5. $9 - k$, for $k = 2$ _____

6. $63 \div p$, for $p = 7$ _____

7. $2 + n$, for $n = 3$ _____

8. $3m$, for $m = 11$ _____

9. $10 - r + 5$, for $r = 9$ _____

10. $m + n \div 6$, for $m = 12$ and $n = 18$ _____

11. $1{,}221 \div x$, for $x = 37$ _____

12. $10 - x$, for $x = 3$ _____

13. $4m + 3$, for $m = 5$ _____

14. $35 - 3x$, for $x = 10$ _____

15. $851 - p$, for $p = 215$ _____

16. $18a - 9b$, for $a = 12$ and $b = 15$ _____

17. $3ab - c$, for $a = 4$, $b = 2$, and $c = 5$ _____

18. $\frac{ab}{2} + 4c$, for $a = 6$, $b = 5$, and $c = 3$ _____

19. $\frac{rst}{3}$, for $r = 9$, $s = 2$, and $t = 4$ _____

20. $x(y + 5) - z$, for $x = 3$, $y = 2$, and $z = 7$ _____

21. Elliot is 58 years old.

   a. Write an expression for the number of years by which Elliot's age

   exceeds that of his daughter, who is y years old. _____

   b. If his daughter is 25, how much older is Elliot? _____

22. A tree grows 5 in. each year.

   a. Write an expression for the tree's height after x years. _____

   b. When the tree is 36 years old, how tall will it be? _____

Practice 1-4 Integers and Absolute Value

Graph each set of numbers on a number line. Then order the numbers from least to greatest.

1. $-4, -8, 5$

_____

2. $3, -3, -2$

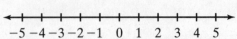

_____

3. $0, -9, -5$

_____

4. $-7, -1, -6$

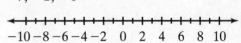

_____

Write an integer to represent each quantity.

5. 5 degrees below zero _____

6. 2,000 ft above sea level _____

7. a loss of 12 yd _____

8. 7 strokes under par _____

Simplify each expression.

9. the opposite of -15 _____

10. $|-9|$ _____

11. $-|-25|$ _____

12. the opposite of $|-8|$ _____

13. $-|-31|$ _____

14. $|847|$ _____

Write the integer represented by each point on the number line.

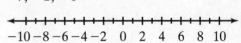

15. A _____

16. B _____

17. C _____

18. D _____

19. E _____

Compare. Use >, <, or = to complete each statement.

20. $-3 \boxed{} 4$

21. $5 \boxed{} 1$

22. $-2 \boxed{} -6$

23. $7 \boxed{} |8|$

24. $|-2| \boxed{} |2|$

25. $|-1| \boxed{} -6$

26. $|4| \boxed{} |-5|$

27. $0 \boxed{} |-7|$

▰▰▰ *Practice 1-5* *Adding Integers*

Write a numerical expression for each of the following. Then find the sum.

1. climb up 26 steps, then climb down 9 steps

_____

2. earn $100, spend $62, earn $35, spend $72

_____

Find each sum.

3. $-8 + (-3)$

4. $6 + (-6)$

5. $-12 + (-17)$

6. $9 + (-11)$

7. $-4 + (-6)$

8. $18 + (-17)$

9. $-8 + 8 + (-11)$

10. $12 + (-7) + 3 + (-8)$

11. $-15 + 7 + 15$

12. $0 + (-11)$

13. $6 + (-5) + (-4)$

14. $-5 + (-16) + 5 + 8 + 16$

Without adding, tell whether each sum is positive, negative, or zero.

15. $192 + (-129)$

16. $-417 + (-296)$

17. $-175 + 87$

Evaluate each expression for $n = -12$.

18. $n + 8$

19. $n + (-5)$

20. $12 + n$

Compare. Write >, <, or = to complete each statement.

21. $-7 + 5 \;\boxed{}\; 3 + (-6)$

22. $4 + (-9) \;\boxed{}\; 6 + (-7) + (-4)$

23. An elevator went up 15 floors, down 9 floors, up 11 floors, and down 19 floors. Find the net change. _____

24. The price of a share of stock started the day at $37. During the day it went down $3, up $1, down $7, and up $4. What was the price of a share at the end of the day?

_____

Practice 1-6 *Subtracting Integers*

Use rules to find each difference.

1. 8 − 12 _____

2. 13 − 6 _____

3. 9 − (−12) _____

4. 57 − 39 _____

5. −173 − 162 _____

6. 71 − (123) _____

7. 51 − 89 _____

8. −222 − (−117) _____

9. 843 − 677 _____

10. −98 − 183 _____

11. 366 − (−429) _____

12. −83 − (−48) − 65 _____

Find each difference.

13. 6 − 9 _____

14. 14 − 8 _____

15. −15 − 3 _____

16. −25 − 25 _____

17. −16 − (−16) _____

18. 32 − (−17) − 32 _____

Round each number. Then estimate each sum or difference.

19. −57 + (−98) _____

20. 448 − 52 _____

21. −191 + (−511) _____

22. −361 − (−58) _____

23. 888 + 1,177 _____

24. −484 − 1,695 _____

Write a numerical expression for each phrase. Then simplify.

25. A balloon goes up 2,300 ft, then goes down 600 ft.

_____

26. You lose $50, then spend $35.

_____

27. The Glasers had $317 in their checking account. They wrote checks for $74, $132, and $48. What is their checking account balance?

_____

Practice 1-7 *Inductive Reasoning*

Write a rule for each pattern. Find the next three numbers in each pattern.

1. 3, 6, 9, 12, 15, _____ , _____ , _____

Rule: _____

_____

2. 1, 2, 4, 8, 16, _____ , _____ , _____

Rule: _____

_____

3. 6, 7, 14, 15, 30, 31, _____ , _____ , _____

Rule: _____

_____

4. 34, 27, 20, 13, 6, _____ , _____ , _____

Rule: _____

_____

Is each statement correct or incorrect? If it is incorrect, give a counterexample.

5. All roses are red

_____

6. A number is divisible by 4 if its last two digits are divisible by 4.

_____

7. The difference of two numbers is always less than at least one of the numbers.

_____

Describe the next figure in each pattern. Then draw the figure.

8.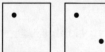

_____

9.

_____

10.

_____

11.

_____

Practice 1-8 *Look for a Pattern*

Solve using any strategy.

1. Each row in a window display of floppy disk cartons contains two more boxes than the row above. The first row has one box.
   a. Complete the table.

Row Number	1	2	3	4	5	6
Boxes in the row						
Total boxes in the display						

   b. Describe the pattern in the numbers you wrote.

   _____

   _____

   c. Find the number of rows in a display containing the given number of boxes.

   81 _____   144 _____   400 _____

   d. Describe how you can use the number of boxes in the display to calculate the number of rows.

   _____

   _____

2. A computer multiplied nine 100 times. You can use patterns to find the ones' digit of the product.

   $$9 \times 9 \times 9 \times 9 \times \cdots \times 9$$

   100 times

   a. Find the ones' digit when nine is multiplied:

   1 time _____   2 times _____   3 times _____   4 times _____

   b. Describe the pattern. _____

   _____

   _____

   _____

   c. What is the ones' digit of the computer product? _____

3. Use the method of Exercise 2 to find the ones' digit of the product when 4 is multiplied by itself 100 times. _____

Practice 1-9 *Multiplying and Dividing Integers*

Use repeated addition, patterns, or rules to find each product or quotient.

1. $23 \cdot 16$

2. $8 \cdot 7(-6)$

3. $-17 \cdot 3$

4. $-24 \div 4$

5. $-65 \div 5$

6. $117 \div (-1)$

7. $-30 \div (-6)$

8. $-21 \div (-3)$

9. $63 \div (-21)$

10. $5(-1)(-9)$

11. $-6(-3) \cdot 2$

12. $-3 \cdot 7(-2)$

13. $\frac{1,512}{-42}$

14. $\frac{-4,875}{-65}$

15. $\frac{-15(-3)}{-9}$

Compare. Use >, <, or = to complete each statement.

16. $-7(5)$ ☐ $-6 \cdot (-6)$

17. $-20 \cdot (-5)$ ☐ $10 \cdot |-10|$

18. $3(-6)$ ☐ $-3(6)$

19. $121 \div (-11)$ ☐ $-45 \div (-6)$

20. $-40 \div 8$ ☐ $40 \div (-8)$

21. $-54 \div 9$ ☐ $21 \div (-3)$

For each group, find the average.

22. temperatures: $6°, -15°, -24°, 3°, -25°$ _____

23. bank balances: $52, -$7, $20, -$63, -82 _____

24. stock price changes: $6, -$6, -$9, $1, 3 _____

25. golf scores: $-2, 0, 3, -2, -3, 1, -4$ _____

26. elevations (ft): $-120, 168, -60, -42, -36$ _____

Write a multiplication or division sentence to answer the question.

27. The temperature dropped $4°$ each hour for 3 hours. What was the total change in temperature?

_____

Practice 1-10 *The Coordinate Plane*

Graph each point.

1. $A(-2, 2)$
2. $B(0, 3)$
3. $C(-3, 0)$
4. $D(2, 3)$
5. $E(-1, -2)$
6. $F(4, -2)$

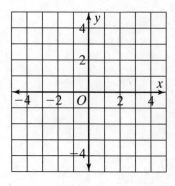

Write the coordinates of each point.

7. A _____
8. B _____

9. C _____
10. D _____

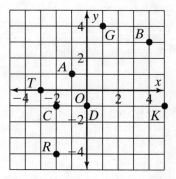

In which quadrant or on what axis does each point fall?

11. A _____
12. B _____

13. C _____
14. D _____

Name the point with the given coordinates.

15. $(1, 4)$ _____
16. $(-3, 0)$ _____

17. $(5, -1)$ _____
18. $(-2, -4)$ _____

Complete using *positive*, or *negative*, or *zero*.

19. In Quadrant II, x is _____ and y is _____.

20. In Quadrant III, x is _____ and y is _____.

21. On the y-axis x is _____.

22. On the x-axis y is _____.

Practice 2-1 *Properties of Numbers*

Mental Math **Simplify each expression.**

1. $4 \cdot 13 \cdot 25$

_____

2. $700 + 127 + 300$

_____

3. $68 + 85 + 32$

_____

4. $2 \cdot 3 \cdot 4 \cdot 5$

_____

5. $-14 + 71 + 29 + (-86)$

_____

6. $125 \cdot 9 \cdot 8$

_____

7. $20 \cdot 7 \cdot 5$

_____

8. $217 + 545 - 17$

_____

9. $39 + 27 + 11$

_____

10. $4 \cdot 12 \cdot 250$

_____

11. $19 + 0 + (-9)$

_____

12. $-6 \cdot 1 \cdot 30$

_____

Write the letter of the property shown.

13. $14(mn) = (14m)n$ _____

14. $19 + 11 = 11 + 19$ _____

15. $k \cdot 1 = k$ _____

16. $(x + y) + z = x + (y + z)$ _____

17. $65t = t(65)$ _____

18. $p = 0 + p$ _____

19. $n = 1 \cdot n$ _____

20. $(x + p) + (r + t) = (r + t) + (x + p)$ _____

21. $(h + 0) + 4 = h + 4$ _____

22. $x + yz = x + zy$ _____

a. commutative property of addition
b. associative property of addition
c. commutative property of multiplication
d. associative property of multiplication
e. additive identity
f. multiplicative identity

Mental Math **Evaluate each expression.**

23. $x(yz)$, for $x = 8, y = -9, z = 5$ _____

24. $q + r + s$, for $q = 46, r = 19, s = 54$ _____

25. $a(b)(-c)$, for $a = 7, b = -2, c = 15$ _____

Practice 2-2 The Distributive Property

Write an expression using parentheses for each model. Then multiply.

1. ▯▯▯▯▤ ▯▯▯▯▤ ▯▯▯▯▤   2. ▯▯▯▯▤ ▯▯▯▯▤

_____   _____

Multiply each expression.

3. $6(h - 4)$ _____   4. $(p + 3)5$ _____

5. $-3(x + 8)$ _____   6. $(4 - y)(-9)$ _____

7. $2(7n - 11)$ _____   8. $-10(-a + 5)$ _____

Use the distributive property to simplify.

9. $98 \cdot 7$ _____

10. $9 \cdot 28$ _____

11. $78 \cdot 8$ _____

12. $7(2{,}009)$ _____

13. $899 \cdot 5$ _____

14. $30 \cdot 105$ _____

15. $8 \cdot 5 - 12 \cdot 5$ _____

16. $7 \cdot 10 + 7(-3)$ _____

17. $-4(3) + (-4)(6)$ _____

18. $6(8) + 6(-2)$ _____

Solve using mental math.

19. A shipping container holds 144 boxes. How many boxes can be shipped

   in 4 containers? _____

Practice 2-3 Simplifying Variable Expressions

Simplify each expression.

1. $16 + 7y - 8$

2. $18m - 7 + 12m$

3. $5(3t) - 7(2t)$

4. $2x - 9y + 7x + 20y$

5. $3(9k - 4) - 4(5n - 3)$

6. $6(g - h) - 6(g - h)$

7. $-21(a + 2b) + 14a - 9b$

8. $-7a + 3(a - c) + 5c$

9. $-2(-5)q + (-72)(-q)$

Name the coefficients, any like terms, and any constants.

	Coefficients	Like Terms	Constants
10. $3x + 7$			
11. $4m + (-3n) + n$			
12. $6kp + 9k + kp - 14$			
13. $-8y + 6ab + 7 - 3ba$			
14. $c + 2c + c - 5c + 1$			

Write an expression for each model. Simplify the expression.

15.  _____

16.  _____

Justify each step.

17. $5(n + 4) + 9n = (5n + 20) + 9n$ _____

$= 5n + (20 + 9n)$ _____

$= 5n + (9n + 20)$ _____

$= (5n + 9n) + 20$ _____

$= (5 + 9)n + 20$ _____

$= 14n + 20$ _____

Practice 2-4   *Variables and Equations*

Is the given number a solution of the equation?

1. $9k = 10 - k; -1$ _____

2. $-7r - 15 = -2r; -3$ _____

3. $3g \div (-6) = 5 - g; -10$ _____

4. $-3p = 4p + 35; -5$ _____

5. $8 - e = 2e - 16; 8$ _____

6. $5 - 15s = 8 - 16s; 3$ _____

7. $2(x - 2) - 5x = 5(2 - x); 7$ _____

8. $6a + 3 = 3(3a - 2); 4$ _____

Is each equation true, false, or an open sentence?

9. $14 = x - 9$

10. $8 + 7 = 10$

11. $4 - 15 = 22 - 33$

12. $5 + x = 90 \div 9 + 4$

13. $-7(5 - 9) = 19 - 3(-3)$

14. $6(5 - 8) = 2(10 - 1)$

Write an equation for each sentence. Is each equation true, false, or an open sentence.

15. One fifth of a number n is equal to -7.

16. The product of 13 and -7 is -91.

17. Fifty-four divided by six equals negative nine.

18. Seven less than the product of a number z and 3 is equal to 4.

Write an equation. Is the given value a solution?

19. A truck driver drove 468 miles on Tuesday. That was 132 miles farther than she drove on Monday. Let d represent the distance she drove on Monday. Did she drive 600 miles on Monday?

Practice 2-5   Solving Equations by Adding or Subtracting

Use mental math to solve each equation.

1. $-52 = -52 + k$ _____   **2.** $837 = p + 37$ _____

3. $x - 155 = 15$ _____   **4.** $180 = 80 + n$ _____

5. $2,000 + y = 9,500$ _____   **6.** $81 = x - 19$ _____

7. $111 + f = 100$ _____   **8.** $w - 6 = -16$ _____

Solve each equation.

9. $m - 17 = -8$ _____   **10.** $k - 55 = 67$ _____

11. $-44 + n = 36$ _____   **12.** $-36 = p - 91$ _____

13. $x - 255 = 671$ _____   **14.** $19 = c - (-12)$ _____

15. $x + 14 = 21$ _____   **16.** $31 = p + 17$ _____

17. $-19 = k + 9$ _____   **18.** $87 + y = 19$ _____

19. $36 + n = 75$ _____   **20.** $-176 = h + (-219)$ _____

21. $41 + k = 7$ _____   **22.** $1,523 + c = 2,766$ _____

23. $-88 + z = 0$ _____   **24.** $-33 + (-7) = 29 + m$ _____

25. $t + (-2) = -66$ _____   **26.** $-390 + x = 11 - 67$ _____

27. The combined enrollment in the three grades at Jefferson Middle School is 977. There are 356 students in the seventh grade and 365 in the eighth grade. Write and solve an equation to find how many students are in the ninth grade.

Equation _____

Solution _____

Practice 2-6 Solving Equations by Multiplying or Dividing

Solve each equation.

1. $\frac{k}{-5} = -5$ _____

2. $-3 = \frac{n}{7}$ _____

3. $\frac{x}{12} = 0$ _____

4. $-6 = \frac{m}{-2}$ _____

5. $\frac{y}{-4} = -12$ _____

6. $\frac{s}{30} = 6$ _____

7. $\frac{1}{9}z = 0$ _____

8. $-\frac{m}{55} = 1$ _____

9. $-3x = 18$ _____

10. $-56 = 8y$ _____

11. $8p = -8$ _____

12. $-4s = -32$ _____

13. $14h = 42$ _____

14. $-175 = 25g$ _____

15. $-42 = 6m$ _____

16. $-2x = 34$ _____

17. $\frac{x}{-9} = -11$ _____

18. $216 = 9w$ _____

19. $-17v = -17$ _____

20. $-161 = 23t$ _____

21. $56h = 3{,}136$ _____

22. $20 = \frac{e}{-25}$ _____

23. $4{,}200 = 30x$ _____

24. $\frac{y}{-21} = -21$ _____

25. $\frac{m}{-3} = 21$ _____

26. $4{,}000 = \frac{x}{-40}$ _____

27. A bamboo tree grew 3 in. per day. Write and solve an equation to find how many days d it took the tree to grow 144 in.

Equation: _____ Solution: _____

28. Carl drove 561 miles. His car averages 33 miles per gallon of gas. Write and solve an equation to find how much gas g Carl's car used.

Equation: _____ Solution: _____

For what values of y is each equation true?

29. $-5|y| = -25$

30. $\frac{|y|}{2} = 28$

31. $9|y| = 27$

_____ _____ _____

▰▰ *Practice 2-7* *Try, Test, Revise*

Use the Try, Test, Revise strategy to solve each problem.

1. The length of a rectangle is 9 in. greater than the width. The area is 36 in.^{2} Find the dimensions. _____

Width						
Length						
Area						

2. Shari Williams, a basketball player, scored 30 points on 2-point and 3-point goals. She hit 5 more 2-pointers than 3-pointers. How many of each did she score? _____

3-pointers						
2-pointers						
points						

3. The sums and products of pairs of integers are given. Find each pair of integers.

   a. sum = −12, product = 36 _____

   b. sum = −12, product = 35 _____

   c. sum = −12, product = 32 _____

   d. sum = −12, product = 11 _____

   e. sum = −12, product = 0 _____

4. Jess had 3 more nickels than dimes for a total of $1.50. How many of each coin did he have?

   _____

5. A brush cost $2 more than a comb. The brush and a comb together cost $3.78. Find the cost of each.

   _____

6. The hard-cover edition of a book cost 3 times as much as the paperback edition. Both editions together cost $26.60. Find the cost of each.

   _____

Practice 2-8   Inequalities and Their Graphs

Write an inequality for each sentence.

1. The total t is less than sixteen. _____

2. A number h is not less than 7. _____

3. The price p is less than or equal to $25. _____

4. A number n is negative. _____

Write an inequality for each graph.

5.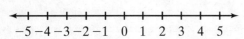

_____

6.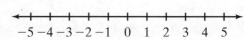

_____

7.
```
←+—+—+—+—+—+—+—⊕—+—+—+→
 −5 −4 −3 −2 −1  0  1  2  3  4  5
```

_____

8.
```
←+—+—●—+—+—+—+—+—+—+—+→
 −5 −4 −3 −2 −1  0  1  2  3  4  5
```

_____

Graph the solutions of each inequality on a number line.

9. $x < -2$

```
←+—+—+—+—+—+—+—+—+—+—+→
 −5 −4 −3 −2 −1  0  1  2  3  4  5
```

10. $y \geq -1$

```
←+—+—+—+—+—+—+—+—+—+—+→
 −5 −4 −3 −2 −1  0  1  2  3  4  5
```

11. $k > 1$

```
←+—+—+—+—+—+—+—+—+—+—+→
 −5 −4 −3 −2 −1  0  1  2  3  4  5
```

12. $p \leq 4$

```
←+—+—+—+—+—+—+—+—+—+—+→
 −5 −4 −3 −2 −1  0  1  2  3  4  5
```

Write an inequality for each situation.

13. Everyone in the class is under 13 years old. Let x be the age of a person in the class.

_____

14. The speed limit is 60 miles per hour. Let s be the speed of a car driving within the limit.

_____

15. You have $4.50 to spend on lunch. Let c be the cost of your lunch.

_____

Name _____ Class _____ Date _____

Practice 2-9 Solving One-Step Inequalities by Adding or Subtracting

Write an inequality for each sentence. Then solve the inequality.

1. Six less than n is less than -4.

_____

2. The sum of a number k and five is greater than or equal to two.

_____

3. Nine more than a number b is greater than negative three.

_____

4. You must be at least 48 inches tall to ride an amusement park ride, and your little sister is 39 inches tall. How many inches i must she grow before she may ride the ride?

_____

5. You need no more than 3,000 calories in a day. You consumed 840 calories at breakfast and 1,150 calories at lunch. How many calories c can you eat for dinner?

_____

Solve each inequality. Graph the solutions.

6. $7 + x \geq 9$ _____

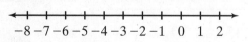

7. $-5 \leq x - 6$ _____

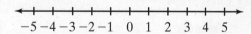

8. $0 \geq x + 12$ _____

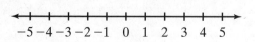

9. $x - 15 \leq -8$ _____

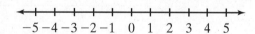

10. $13 + x \geq 13$ _____

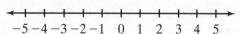

11. $x - 8 > -5$ _____

12. $4 + x < -2$ _____

13. $x - 9 > -11$ _____

14. $x - 6 \leq -1$ _____

15. $-4 + x < -4$ _____

■ Practice 2-10 *Solving One-Step Inequalities by Multiplying or Dividing*

Write an inequality for each sentence. Then solve the inequality.

1. The product of k and -5 is no more than 30.

_____

2. Half of p is at least -7.

_____

3. The product of k and 9 is no more than 18.

_____

4. One-third of p is at least -17.

_____

5. The opposite of g is at least -5.

_____

Solve each inequality.

6. $-5x < 10$ _____   **7.** $\frac{x}{4} > 1$ _____

8. $-8 < -8x$ _____   **9.** $\frac{1}{3}x > -2$ _____

10. $48 \geq -12x$ _____   **11.** $\frac{1}{3}x < -6$ _____

12. $\frac{x}{5} < -4$ _____   **13.** $-x \leq 2$ _____

Determine whether each number is a solution of $7 \geq -3k$.

14. 2 _____   **15.** -2 _____   **16.** 0 _____   **17.** -3 _____

Justify each step.

18. $-5n \geq 45$

$\dfrac{-5n}{-5} \leq \dfrac{45}{-5}$ _____

$n \leq -9$ _____

Practice 3-1 Rounding and Estimating

Estimate using front-end estimation.

1. 6.3 + 8.55

2. 345 + 682

3. 4.60 + 5.53

_____

_____

_____

4. $6.14 + $9.38

5. $39.65 + $25.84

6. 9.71 + 3.94

_____

_____

_____

Estimate by clustering.

7. $7.04 + $5.95 + $6.08 + $5.06 + $6.12

8. 9.3 + 8.7 + 8.91 + 9.052

_____

_____

9. 37.6 + 44.91 + 41 + 39.1

10. 2.357 + 1.874 + 1.956

_____

_____

Estimate by rounding each number to the same place value.

11. 14.66 + 25.19 _____

12. 8.7 + 3.21 + 3.899 _____

13. 194.78 − 12.31 _____

14. $289 − $67.20 _____

15. 800 − 301.47 _____

16. 0.06 + 19.41 _____

Round to the underlined place value.

17. 6.<u>7</u>39 _____

18. 52.1<u>9</u>2 _____

19. <u>0</u>.61 _____

20. 348.5<u>0</u>8 _____

Estimate. State your method (rounding, front-end, or clustering).

21. 91.7 + 88.6 + 89.1 + 92.5 + 90.6 _____

22. 3.9 + 8.1 + 2.06 _____

23. $1.08 + $.95 + $.89 + $1.14 _____

24. 11.56 + 19.43 + 13.40 + 14.39 _____

25. 0.015 + 0.039 + 0.0266 _____

Practice 3-2 Estimating Decimal Products and Quotients

Determine whether each product or quotient is reasonable. If it is not reasonable, find a reasonable result.

1. $62.77(29.8) = 187.0546$

_____

2. $16.132 \div 2.96 = 54.5$

_____

3. $(47.89)(6.193) = 296.5828$

_____

4. $318.274 \div 4.07 = 78.2$

_____

5. $2.65(-0.84) = -0.2226$

_____

6. $-38.6(-1.89) = 7.2954$

_____

7. $6,355 \div 775 = 8.2$

_____

8. $1,444.14 \div 67.8 = 213$

_____

9. $1.839(6.3) = 115.857$

_____

10. $3.276 \div 0.63 = 5.2$

_____

Estimate each product or quotient.

11. $8.73 \cdot 6.01$ _____

12. $11.042(4.56)$ _____

13. $197.4 \cdot 2.85$ _____

14. $675.1 \cdot 0.051$ _____

15. $479.2(3.2)$ _____

16. $712.9 \cdot 0.41$ _____

17. $11.57 \div 3.09$ _____

18. $43.68 \div 8.7$ _____

19. $29.5 \div 5.1$ _____

20. $\$41.09 \div \$6.88$ _____

21. $148.8 \div 9.8$ _____

22. $\$76.77 \div \$24.19$ _____

23. Apples cost $.89 per lb. Estimate the cost of three 5-lb bags. _____

24. You buy 3 dinners that are $6.85 each. Before tax and tip, the total is $25.42. Is this total correct? Explain.

_____

25. You worked 18 hours last week and received $92.70 in your paycheck. Estimate your hourly pay.

_____

Practice 3-3 Mean, Median, and Mode

1. There were 8 judges at a gymnastics competition. Kathleen received these scores for her performance on the uneven parallel bars:
   8.9, 8.7, 8.9, 9.2, 8.8, 8.2, 8.9, 8.8

   a. Find these statistics: mean _____ median _____ mode _____

   b. Which measure of central tendency best describes the data? Explain.

   _____

   _____

   c. Why do you think that the highest and lowest judge's scores are disregarded in tallying the total score in a gymnastics competition?

   _____

   _____

Find the mean, median, and mode. Round to the nearest tenth where necessary. Identify any outliers.

Data	Mean	Median	Mode	Outliers
2. 8, 15, 9, 7, 4, 5, 9, 11	_____	_____	_____	_____
3. 70, 61, 28, 40, 60, 72, 25, 31, 64, 63	_____	_____	_____	_____
4. 4.9, 5.7, 6.0, 5.3, 4.8, 4.9, 5.3, 4.7, 4.9, 5.6, 5.1	_____	_____	_____	_____
5. 271, 221, 234, 240, 271, 234, 213, 253, 155	_____	_____	_____	_____
6. 0, 2, 3, 3, 3, 4, 4, 5	_____	_____	_____	_____

Use the data in the table. Round to the nearest tenth where necessary.

Peak	Height (ft)
Mont Blanc	15,771
Monte Rosa	15,203
Dom	14,911
Liskamm	14,852
Weisshom	14,780

7. What is the mean height of the five highest European mountains? _____

8. What is the median height? _____

9. Is any of the heights an outlier? Explain.

   _____

Practice 3-4 Using Formulas

Use the formula $P = 2l + 2w$. Find the perimeter of each rectangle.

1. _____ **2.** _____ **3.** _____

9 m (rectangle, 4.5 m)	5.2 ft (rectangle, 1.3 ft)	12.9 cm (rectangle, 4.7 cm)

Use the formula $A = lw$. Find the area of each rectangle above.

4. _____ **5.** _____ **6.** _____

7. Use the formula $d = rt$ to find how far each animal in the table can travel in 5 seconds.

Animal	Speed (ft/s)	Distance in 5 s (ft)
Pronghorn antelope	89.5	
Wildebeest	73.3	
Gray fox	61.6	
Wart hog	44.0	
Wild turkey	22.0	
Chicken	13.2	

8. While vacationing on the Mediterranean Sea, Angie recorded the temperature several times during a 24-hour period. She used a thermometer in the lobby of her hotel. It was a beautiful day. Use the formula $F = 1.8C + 32$ to change the temperatures Angie recorded from Celsius to Fahrenheit.

Time	Temperature (°C)	Temperature (°F)
4:00 A.M.	19	
8:00 A.M.	22	
12:00 P.M.	30	
4:00 P.M.	28	
8:00 P.M.	24	
12:00 A.M.	20	

Practice 3-5 Solving Equations by Adding or Subtracting Decimals

Solve each equation.

1. $3.8 = n - 3.62$

_____

2. $x - 19.7 = -17.48$

_____

3. $12.5 = t - 3.55$

_____

4. $k - 263.48 = -381.09$

_____

5. $9.36 + k = 14.8$

_____

6. $-22 = p + 13.7$

_____

7. $y + 3.85 = 2.46$

_____

8. $-13.8 = h + 15.603$

_____

9. $y - 48.763 = 0$

_____

10. $6.21 = e + (-3.48)$

_____

11. $x + (-0.0025) = 0.0024$

_____

12. $-58.109 = v - 47.736$

_____

13. $x + 82.7 = 63.5$

_____

14. $-0.08 = f + 0.07$

_____

15. $0 = a + 27.98$

_____

16. $117.345 + m = 200$

_____

17. $z - 81.6 = -81.6$

_____

18. $5.4 = t + (-6.1)$

_____

19. $-4.095 + b = 18.665$

_____

20. $4.87 = n + 0.87$

_____

Use mental math to solve each equation.

21. $k + 23.7 = 23.7$

_____

22. $5.63 = n + 1.63$

_____

23. $x - 3.2 = 4.1$

_____

24. $p - 0.7 = 9.3$

_____

25. $6.75 + c = 12.95$

_____

26. $-1.09 = j - 4.99$

_____

Practice 3-6 Solving Equations by Multiplying or Dividing Decimals

Use mental math to solve each equation.

1. $0.7h = 4.2$ _____

2. $\frac{x}{2.5} = -3$ _____

3. $38.7 = -100k$ _____

4. $-45.6e = -4.56$ _____

Solve each equation.

5. $\frac{p}{2.9} = 0.55$ _____

6. $9.1 = \frac{x}{-0.7}$ _____

7. $-6.4 = \frac{y}{8.5}$ _____

8. $\frac{k}{-1.2} = -0.07$ _____

9. $277.4 = \frac{n}{3.5}$ _____

10. $\frac{e}{-0.76} = 2,809$ _____

11. $\frac{a}{27} = -32.3$ _____

12. $\frac{p}{-1.52} = -3,600$ _____

13. $-9k = 2.34$ _____

14. $-12.42 = 0.03p$ _____

15. $-7.2y = 61.2$ _____

16. $-0.1035 = 0.23n$ _____

17. $1.5m = 3.03$ _____

18. $-0.007h = 0.2002$ _____

19. $8.13t = -100.812$ _____

20. $0.546 = 0.42y$ _____

Write an equation for each sentence. Solve for the variable.

21. The opposite of seventy-five hundredths times some number n equals twenty-four thousandths. Find the value of n.

_____

22. A number n divided by -3.88 equals negative two thousand. Find the value of n.

_____

23. Four hundredths times some number n equals thirty-three and four tenths. Find the value of n.

_____

24. The product of some number n and -0.26 equals 169.39. Find the value of n.

_____

Practice 3-7 *Using the Metric System*

Write the metric unit that makes each statement true.

1. 7.84 cm = 78.4 _____

2. 423 m = 0.423 _____

3. 2.8 m = 280 _____

4. 6.5 km = 650,000 _____

Complete each statement.

5. 3.4 cm = _____ mm

6. 197.5 cm = _____ m

7. 7 L = _____ mL

8. 5,247 mg = _____ g

9. 87 g = _____ kg

10. 9,246 mL = _____ L

Choose a reasonable estimate. Explain your choice.

11. The amount of water a cup would hold: 250 mL   250 L

_____

12. The mass of a bag of apples: 2 g   2 kg

_____

13. The height of your kitchen table: 68 cm   68 m

_____

Choose an appropriate metric unit. Explain your choice.

14. distance between two cities

_____

15. the mass of a pencil

_____

16. the capacity of an automobile's gas tank

_____

17. One Olympic event is the 1,500-meter run. How many kilometers is this?

_____

18. A fish pond holds 2,500 liters of water. How many kiloliters is this?

_____

◾ *Practice 3-8* *Simplify a Problem*

Solve using any strategy.

1. A house-number manufacturer sold numbers to retail stores for $.09 per digit. A hardware store bought enough digits for two of every house number from 1 to 999. How many digits did the store purchase for house numbers:

   a. 1–9 _____   **b.** 10–99 _____   **c.** 100–999 _____

   d. Find the total cost of the house numbers. _____

2. A tic-tac-toe diagram uses 2 vertical lines and 2 horizontal lines to create 9 spaces. How many spaces can you create using:

   a. 1 vertical line and 1 horizontal line _____

   b. 2 vertical lines and 1 horizontal line _____

   c. 3 vertical lines and 3 horizontal line _____

   d. 4 vertical lines and 5 horizontal lines _____

   e. 17 vertical lines and 29 horizontal lines _____

3. Each side of each triangle in the figure has length 1 cm. The perimeter (the distance around) the first triangle is 3 cm. Find the perimeter of the figure formed by connecting:

   a. 2 triangles _____   **b.** 3 triangles _____

   c. 4 triangles _____   **d.** 50 triangles _____

4. At the inauguration, the President was honored with a 21-gun salute. The report from each gunshot lasted 1 s. Four seconds elapsed between shots. How long did the salute last?

   _____

5. Bernie began building a model airplane on day 7 of his summer vacation and finished building it on day 65. He worked on the plane each day. How many days did it take?

   _____

Practice 4-1 Divisibility and Factors

List all the factors of each number.

1. 12 _____

2. 45 _____

3. 41 _____

4. 54 _____

5. 48 _____

6. 100 _____

7. 117 _____

Test whether each number is divisible by 2, 3, 5, 9, and 10.

8. 215 _____ **9.** 432 _____

10. 770 _____ **11.** 1,011 _____

12 975 _____ **13.** 2,070 _____

14. 3,707 _____ **15.** 5,715 _____

Write the missing digit to make each number divisible by 9.

16. 7☐1 **17.** 2,2☐2 **18.** 88,☐12

19. There are four different digits which, when inserted in the blank space in the number 4☐5, make the number divisible by 3. Write them.

_____

20. There are two different digits which, when inserted in the blank space in the number 7,16☐, make the number divisible by 5. Write them.

_____

21. There are five different digits which, when inserted in the blank space in the number 99,99☐, make the number divisible by 2. Write them.

_____

Practice 4-2 Exponents

Evaluate each expression.

1. m^4, for $m = 5$ _____

2. $(5a)^3$, for $a = -1$ _____

3. $-(2p)^2$, for $p = 7$ _____

4. $-n^6$, for $n = 2$ _____

5. b^6 for, $b = -1$ _____

6. $(e - 2)^3$, for $e = 11$ _____

7. $(6 + h^2)^2$, for $h = 3$ _____

8. $x^2 + 3x - 7$, for $x = -4$ _____

9. $y^3 - 2y^2 + 3y - 4$, for $y = 5$ _____

Write using exponents.

10. $3 \cdot 3 \cdot 3 \cdot 3$ _____

11. $k \cdot k \cdot k \cdot k \cdot k$ _____

12. $(-9)(-9)(-9)m \cdot m \cdot m$ _____

13. $g \cdot g \cdot g \cdot g \cdot h$ _____

14. $7 \cdot a \cdot a \cdot b \cdot b \cdot b$ _____

15. $-8 \cdot m \cdot n \cdot n \cdot 2 \cdot m \cdot m$ _____

16. $d \cdot (-3) \cdot e \cdot e \cdot d \cdot (-3) \cdot e$ _____

Simplify each expression.

17. $(-2)^3$ and -2^3 _____

18. 0^{12} _____

19. 2^8 and 4^4 _____

20. $-5^2 + 4 \cdot 2^3$ _____

21. $3(8 - 6)^2$ _____

22. $-6^2 + 2 \cdot 3^2$ _____

23. $(-2)(-5)^2(3)$ _____

24. $24 + (11 - 3)^2 \div 4$ _____

25. $(17 - 3)^2 \div (4^2 - 3^2)$ _____

26. $(5 + 10)^2 \div 5^2$ _____

27. $4^3 \div (2^5 - 4^2)$ _____

28. $(-1)^5 \cdot (2^4 - 13)^2$ _____

Practice 4-3 Prime Factorization and Greatest Common Factor

Find each GCF.

1. $8, 12$ _____ **2.** $36, 54$ _____

3. $63, 81$ _____ **4.** $69, 92$ _____

5. $15, 28$ _____ **6.** $21, 35$ _____

7. $30m, 36n$ _____ **8.** $75x^3y^2, 100xy$ _____

9. $15, 24, 30$ _____ **10.** $48, 80, 128$ _____

11. $36hk^3, 60k^2m, 84k^4n$ _____ **12.** $2mn, 4m^2n^2$ _____

Is each number prime, composite, or neither? For each composite, write the prime factorization.

13. 75 _____ **14.** 152 _____

15. 432 _____ **16.** 588 _____

17. 160 _____ **18.** 108 _____

19. 19 _____ **20.** 143 _____

21. 531 _____ **22.** 369 _____

23. 83 _____ **24.** 137 _____

25. The numbers 3, 5, and 7 are factors of n. Find four other factors of n besides 1.

_____

26. For which expressions is the GCF $8x$?

    A. $2xy$ and $4x^2$ **B.** $16x^2$ and $24xy$ **C.** $8x^3$ and $4x$ **D.** $24x^2$ and $48x^3$

Practice 4-4 Simplifying Fractions

Write in simplest form.

1. $\frac{10}{15}$ _____

2. $\frac{18}{36}$ _____

3. $\frac{27}{36}$ _____

4. $\frac{12}{15}$ _____

5. $\frac{26}{39}$ _____

6. $\frac{7b}{9b}$ _____

7. $\frac{16y^3}{20y^4}$ _____

8. $\frac{8x}{10y}$ _____

9. $\frac{6xy}{16y}$ _____

10. $\frac{24n^2}{28n}$ _____

11. $\frac{abc}{10abc}$ _____

12. $\frac{30hxy}{54kxy}$ _____

13. $\frac{mn^2}{pm^5n}$ _____

14. $\frac{5jh}{15jh^3}$ _____

15. $\frac{12h^3k}{16h^2k^2}$ _____

16. $\frac{20s^2t^3}{16st^5}$ _____

Find two fractions equivalent to each fraction.

17. $\frac{1}{4}$ _____

18. $\frac{2}{3}$ _____

19. $\frac{3}{5}$ _____

20. $\frac{3}{18}$ _____

21. $\frac{8k}{16k}$ _____

22. $\frac{3m}{8n}$ _____

23. $\frac{5pq}{10p^2q^3}$ _____

24. $\frac{3s^2t^2}{7r}$ _____

25. Monty completed 18 passes in 30 attempts. What fraction of his passes did Monty complete? Write in simplest form.

_____

26. Five new state quarters will be issued by the United States mint this year. What fraction of the states will have quarters issued this year?

_____

Name _____ Class _____ Date _____

Practice 4-5 Account for All Possibilities

Solve each problem by accounting for all possibilities.

1. A baseball team has 4 pitchers and 3 catchers. How many different pitcher-catcher combinations are possible? One way to solve this problem is to make a list like the one started below. Finish the list.

   P1-C1   P2-C1
   P1-C2   P2-C2

   _____   _____

   _____   _____

   _____   _____

   _____   _____

2. The baseball team has 2 first basemen, 3 second basemen, and 2 third basemen. How many combinations of the three positions are possible?

   _____

3. A quarter is tossed 3 times. In how many different orders can heads and tails be tossed?

   _____

4. A quarter is tossed 4 times. In how many different orders can heads and tails be tossed?

   _____

5. Curtains are manufactured in 3 different styles and 5 different colors.
   a. How many different style-color combinations are possible?

   _____

   b. The curtains are produced in 2 different fabrics. How many different style-color-fabric combinations are possible?

   _____

Practice Workbook   33   *Pre-Algebra*

Practice 4-6 Rational Numbers

Graph the rational numbers below on the same number line.

1. $\frac{3}{4}$ **2.** $-\frac{1}{4}$ **3.** -0.5 **4.** 0.3

```
←―┼――┼――┼――┼――┼――┼――┼――→
 -1.0  -0.5   0   0.5   1.0
```

Evaluate. Write in simplest form.

5. $\frac{x}{y}$, for $x = 12, y = 21$ _____

6. $\frac{n}{n + p}$, for $n = 9, p = 6$ _____

7. $\frac{k}{k^2 + 4}$, for $k = 6$ _____

8. $\frac{x - y}{-21}$, for $x = -2, y = 5$ _____

9. $\frac{m}{-n}$, for $m = 6, n = 7$ _____

10. $\frac{x(xy - 8)}{60}$, for $x = 3, y = 9$ _____

Write three fractions equivalent to each fraction.

11. $\frac{5}{7}$ _____

12. $\frac{22}{33}$ _____

13. $\frac{24}{30}$ _____

14. $\frac{6}{16}$ _____

15. Which of the following rational numbers are equal to $-\frac{17}{10}$?

$-17, -1.7, -\frac{34}{20}, 0.17$ _____

16. Which of the following rational numbers are equal to $\frac{3}{5}$?

$\frac{12}{20}, \frac{-3}{-5}, 0.3, \frac{6}{10}$ _____

17. Which of the following rational numbers are equal to $\frac{12}{15}$?

$\frac{4}{5}, \frac{40}{50}, -\frac{8}{10}, \frac{8}{10}$ _____

18. The weight w of an object in pounds is related to its distance d from the center of Earth by the equation $w = \frac{320}{d^2}$, where d is in thousands of miles. How much does the object weigh at sea level which is about 4,000 miles from the center of Earth?

_____

Name _____ Class _____ Date _____

Practice 4-7 Exponents and Multiplication

Complete each equation.

1. $9^3 \cdot 9^{\underline{}} = 9^7$

2. $6^8 \cdot 6^{\underline{}} = 6^{17}$

3. $n^{\underline{}} \cdot n^5 = n^{15}$

4. $(a^{\underline{}})^8 = a^{24}$

5. $(c^4)^{\underline{}} = c^{12}$

6. $r^{\underline{}} \cdot r^{12} = r^{20}$

Simplify each expression.

7. $(z^3)^5$ _____

8. $-(m^4)^3$ _____

9. $(-3^2)^3$ _____

10. $(x^3)(x^4)$ _____

11. $y^4 \cdot y^5$ _____

12. $(-y^5)(y^2)$ _____

13. $(3y^2)(2y^3)$ _____

14. $3x^{12} \cdot 2x^3$ _____

15. $m^{30} \cdot m^{12}$ _____

16. $(x^4)(y^2)(x^2)$ _____

17. $(-6x^7)(-9x^{12})$ _____

18. $(h^4)^4$ _____

Find the area of each rectangle.

19.

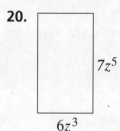

p^2

$3p^4$

20.

$7z^5$

$6z^3$

_____   _____

Compare. Use >, <, or = to complete each statement.

21. $(4^3)^2$ ▢ $(4^2)^3$

22. $5^3 \cdot 5^4$ ▢ 5^{10}

23. $(3^5)^4$ ▢ 3^{10}

24. 3^4 ▢ 9^2

25. $(9^7)^9$ ▢ $(9^8)^8$

26. $4^2 \cdot 4^3$ ▢ 4^5

27. $(6^2)^2$ ▢ $3^4 \cdot 2^4$

28. $5^2 \cdot 5^6$ ▢ 5^7

29. $(8^2)^2$ ▢ $(8^2)^3$

Practice 4-8 *Exponents and Division*

Complete each equation.

1. $\frac{8^n}{8^7} = 8^2$, $n =$ _____

2. $\frac{12x^5}{4x} = 3x^n$, $n =$ _____

3. $\frac{1}{h^5} = h^n$, $n =$ _____

4. $\frac{p^n}{p^8} = p^{-6}$, $n =$ _____

5. $\frac{1}{81} = 3^n$, $n =$ _____

6. $\frac{12^4}{12^n} = 1$, $n =$ _____

Simplify each expression.

7. $\frac{a^3}{a^7}$ _____

8. $\frac{j^5}{j^6}$ _____

9. $\frac{x^7}{x^7}$ _____

10. $\frac{k^5}{k^9}$ _____

11. $\frac{9x^8}{12x^5}$ _____

12. $\frac{2f^{10}}{f^5}$ _____

13. $\frac{3y^4}{6y^{-4}}$ _____

14. n^{-5} _____

15. $\frac{3xy^4}{9xy}$ _____

16. $(-15)^0$ _____

17. $\frac{15h^6k^3}{5hk^2}$ _____

18. $4b^{-6}$ _____

Write each expression without a fraction bar.

19. $\frac{a^7}{a^{10}}$ _____

20. $\frac{4x^2y}{2x^3}$ _____

21. $\frac{x^3y^4}{x^9y^2}$ _____

22. $\frac{12mn}{12m^3n^5}$ _____

23. $\frac{16s^2t^4}{8s^5t^3}$ _____

24. $\frac{21e^4f^2}{7e^2}$ _____

25. Write three different quotients that equal 4^{-5}.

_____

Practice 4-9 Scientific Notation

Write each number in standard notation.

1. 3.77×10^4 _____

2. 8.5×10^3 _____

3. 9.002×10^{-5} _____

4. 1.91×10^{-3} _____

Write each number in scientific notation.

5. Pluto is about 3,653,000,000 mi from the sun. _____

6. There are 63,360 in. in a mile. _____

7. At its closest, Mercury is about 46,000,000 km from the sun. _____

8. 77,250,000 _____

9. 526,000 _____

10. 8 billion _____

11. 8,100,000 _____

12. 0.00000073 _____

13. 0.000903 _____

Multiply. Express each result in scientific notation.

14. $(2 \times 10^5)(3 \times 10^2)$

15. $(1.5 \times 10^5)(4 \times 10^9)$

16. $(6 \times 10^{-4})(1.2 \times 10^{-3})$

17. $(5 \times 10^3)(1.7 \times 10^{-5})$

Order from least to greatest.

18. $72 \times 10^5, 6.9 \times 10^6, 23 \times 10^5$

19. $19 \times 10^{-3}, 2.5 \times 10^{-4}, 1.89 \times 10^{-4}$

20. An ounce is 0.00003125 tons. Write this number in scientific notation.

21. A century is 3,153,600,000 seconds. Write this number in scientific notation.

Name _____ Class _____ Date _____

Practice 5-1 Comparing and Ordering Fractions

Compare. Use >, <, or = to complete each statement.

1. $\frac{2}{3}$ ☐ $\frac{7}{9}$

2. $\frac{3}{5}$ ☐ $\frac{7}{10}$

3. $-\frac{3}{4}$ ☐ $-\frac{13}{16}$

4. $\frac{9}{21}$ ☐ $\frac{6}{14}$

5. $-\frac{2}{8}$ ☐ $-\frac{7}{32}$

6. $\frac{7}{9}$ ☐ $-\frac{8}{9}$

7. $\frac{5}{8}$ ☐ $\frac{7}{12}$

8. $-\frac{4}{5}$ ☐ $-\frac{7}{8}$

9. $-\frac{4}{18}$ ☐ $-\frac{6}{27}$

10. $\frac{8}{17}$ ☐ $-\frac{3}{8}$

11. $\frac{4}{7}$ ☐ $2\frac{4}{7}$

12. $\frac{-9}{-11}$ ☐ $\frac{9}{11}$

13. $\frac{1}{3}$ ☐ $-\frac{3}{9}$

14. $-\frac{12}{6}$ ☐ $-\frac{9}{3}$

15. $-\frac{5}{10}$ ☐ $\frac{-3}{-4}$

Find the LCM of each group of numbers or expressions.

16. $7, 21$ _____

17. $24, 32$ _____

18. $15, 50$ _____

19. $9a^3b, 18abc$ _____

20. $28xy^2, 42x^2y$ _____

21. $9, 12, 16$ _____

22. A quality control inspector in an egg factory checks every forty-eighth egg for cracks and every fifty-fourth egg for weight. What is the number of the first egg each day that the inspector checks for both qualities?

_____

23. A stock sold for $3\frac{5}{8}$ one day and $3\frac{1}{2}$ the next. Did the value of the stock go up or down? Explain.

_____

24. Marissa needs $2\frac{2}{3}$ yards of ribbon for a wall-hanging she wants to make. She has $2\frac{3}{4}$ yards. Does she have enough ribbon? Explain.

_____

Order from least to greatest.

25. $\frac{2}{3}, \frac{3}{4}, \frac{1}{2}$

26. $\frac{2}{5}, \frac{1}{3}, \frac{3}{7}, \frac{4}{9}$

27. $\frac{8}{11}, \frac{9}{10}, \frac{7}{8}, \frac{3}{4}$

_____   _____   _____

Practice 5-2 *Fractions and Decimals*

Write as a fraction or mixed number in simplest form.

1. 0.4 _____

2. 0.75 _____

3. 0.16 _____

4. 2.34 _____

5. 0.09 _____

6. 8.8 _____

Write each fraction or mixed number as a decimal.

7. $\frac{17}{20}$ _____

8. $\frac{7}{8}$ _____

9. $-\frac{9}{16}$ _____

10. $3\frac{1}{8}$ _____

11. $6\frac{9}{32}$ _____

12. $2\frac{87}{125}$ _____

13. $\frac{13}{25}$ _____

14. $4\frac{31}{50}$ _____

15. $-\frac{7}{12}$ _____

16. $\frac{4}{9}$ _____

17. $\frac{5}{18}$ _____

18. $\frac{15}{11}$ _____

Order from least to greatest

19. $0.4, \frac{3}{5}, \frac{1}{2}, \frac{3}{10}$ _____

20. $-\frac{3}{8}, -\frac{3}{4}, -0.38, -0.6$ _____

21. $\frac{1}{4}, -\frac{1}{5}, 0.2, \frac{2}{5}$ _____

22. Write an improper fraction with the greatest possible value using each of the digits 5, 7, and 9 once. Write this as a mixed number and as a decimal.

_____

Write each decimal as a fraction or mixed number in simplest form.

23. $10.0\overline{7}$ _____

24. 3.44 _____

25. $-4.\overline{27}$ _____

26. 0.09 _____

27. 0.375 _____

28. $0.2\overline{43}$ _____

Compare. Use <, >, or = to complete each statement.

29. $\frac{5}{6}$ ☐ 0.8

30. $\frac{7}{11}$ ☐ 0.65

31. $4.\overline{2}$ ☐ $4\frac{2}{9}$

32. $-\frac{3}{11}$ ☐ -0.25

33. $0.\overline{80}$ ☐ $\frac{80}{99}$

34. -0.43 ☐ $-\frac{7}{16}$

Practice 5-3 Adding and Subtracting Fractions

Find each sum or difference.

1. $\frac{2}{3} + \frac{1}{6}$ _____

2. $\frac{5}{8} - \frac{1}{4}$ _____

3. $2 - \frac{5}{7}$ _____

4. $1\frac{1}{2} - 2\frac{4}{5}$ _____

5. $\frac{1}{4} - \frac{1}{3}$ _____

6. $5\frac{7}{8} + 3\frac{5}{12}$ _____

7. $\frac{x}{3} + \frac{x}{5}$ _____

8. $\frac{2n}{5} + \left(-\frac{n}{6}\right)$ _____

9. $\frac{7}{12} - \frac{3}{12}$ _____

10. $3\frac{1}{5} + 2\frac{2}{5}$ _____

11. $1\frac{5}{8} - 1\frac{1}{8}$ _____

12. $\frac{3}{5y} + \frac{1}{5y}$ _____

13. $\frac{9}{16} + \frac{3}{4}$ _____

14. $2\frac{7}{10} - 3\frac{7}{20}$ _____

15. $3\frac{5}{6} + 2\frac{3}{4}$ _____

16. $-1\frac{2}{3} + \left(-2\frac{1}{4}\right)$ _____

Find each sum using mental math.

17. $3\frac{3}{8} + 2\frac{1}{8} + 1\frac{3}{8}$ _____

18. $6\frac{7}{12} + 4\frac{5}{12}$ _____

19. $8\frac{3}{16} + 2\frac{5}{16} + 4\frac{7}{16}$ _____

20. $7\frac{9}{10} + 3\frac{3}{10}$ _____

Estimate each sum or difference.

21. $13\frac{4}{5} - 2\frac{9}{10}$ _____

22. $18\frac{3}{8} + 11\frac{6}{7}$ _____

23. $23\frac{6}{13} + 32\frac{7}{8}$ _____

24. $26\frac{9}{10} + 72\frac{5}{6}$ _____

Use prime factors to simplify each expression.

25. $\frac{7}{30} - \frac{29}{75}$ _____

26. $\frac{3}{14} + \frac{17}{63}$ _____

27. $\frac{5}{42} + \frac{5}{12}$ _____

28. $2\frac{5}{6} - 2\frac{5}{22}$ _____

29. $4\frac{4}{15} + 2\frac{4}{39}$ _____

30. $3\frac{5}{9} - 2\frac{11}{12}$ _____

Practice 5-4 *Multiplying and Dividing Fractions*

Find each quotient.

1. $\frac{1}{2} \div \frac{5}{8}$ _____

2. $-\frac{5}{24} \div \frac{7}{12}$ _____

3. $\frac{3}{8} \div \frac{6}{7}$ _____

4. $\frac{15}{19} \div \frac{15}{19}$ _____

5. $8 \div \frac{4}{5}$ _____

6. $6\frac{1}{4} \div 2\frac{1}{2}$ _____

7. $5\frac{5}{8} \div 1\frac{1}{4}$ _____

8. $2\frac{1}{3} \div \frac{7}{10}$ _____

9. $\frac{6}{35t} \div \frac{3}{7t}$ _____

10. $1\frac{3}{7} \div \left(-2\frac{1}{7}\right)$ _____

Find each product.

11. $\frac{2}{5} \cdot \frac{3}{7}$ _____

12. $\frac{5}{9} \cdot \frac{3}{5}$ _____

13. $\frac{7}{9} \cdot \frac{6}{13}$ _____

14. $\frac{5}{6} \cdot \left(-1\frac{3}{10}\right)$ _____

15. $-4\frac{2}{3}\left(-5\frac{1}{6}\right)$ _____

16. $2\frac{5}{6}\left(-\frac{2}{5}\right)$ _____

17. $4\frac{7}{8} \cdot 6$ _____

18. $\frac{5x}{7} \cdot \frac{3}{10}$ _____

19. $\frac{9a}{10} \cdot \frac{5}{12a}$ _____

20. $\frac{9t}{16} \cdot \frac{12}{17}$ _____

21. You are making cookies for a bake sale. The recipe calls for $2\frac{3}{4}$ cups of flour. How much flour will you need if you triple the recipe?

_____

22. It took you 1 hour to read $1\frac{3}{8}$ chapters of a novel. At this rate, how many chapters can you read in three hours.

_____

23. A teacher wants to tape sheets of paper together to make a science banner. He wants the banner to be $127\frac{1}{2}$ inches long, and each sheet of paper is $8\frac{1}{2}$ inches wide. How many sheets of paper will he need?

_____

■ *Practice 5-5* *Using Customary Units of* *Measurement*

Use estimation, mental math, or paper and pencil to convert from one unit to the other.

1. 2 gal 2 qt = _____ qt

2. 3 yd = _____ ft

3. 1 ft 8 in. = _____ in.

4. $\frac{3}{5}$ t = _____ lb

5. 30 in. = _____ ft

6. 20 fl oz = _____ c

7. 20 oz = _____ lb

8. $2\frac{1}{2}$ pt = _____ c

9. $1\frac{1}{8}$ lb = _____ oz

10. 7920 ft = _____ mi

Is each measurement reasonable? If not, give a reasonable measurement.

11. A glass of milk holds about 8 pt.

_____

12. A newborn baby weighs about $7\frac{1}{2}$ oz.

_____

13. A phonebook is $\frac{3}{4}$ ft wide.

_____

Choose an appropriate unit of measure. Explain your choice.

14. weight of a whale

_____

15. sugar in a cookie recipe

_____

16. length of a mouse

_____

Should each item be measured by *length*, *weight*, or *capacity*?

17. amount of soup in a can

_____

18. height of a can

_____

19. heaviness of a can

_____

20. diameter of a can

_____

Practice 5-6 *Work Backward*

Work backward to solve each problem.

1. Manuel's term paper is due on March 31. He began doing research on March 1. He intends to continue doing research for 3 times as long as he has done already. Then he will spend a week writing the paper and the remaining 3 days typing. What day is it? (Assume he will finish typing on March 30.)

   _____

2. A disc jockey must allow time for 24 minutes of commercials every hour, along with 4 minutes for news, 3 minutes for weather, and 2 minutes for public-service announcements. If each record lasts an average of 3 minutes, how many records per hour can the DJ play?

   _____

3. Margaret is reading the 713-page novel *War and Peace*. When she has read twice as many pages as she has read already, she will be 119 pages from the end. What page is she on now?

   _____

4. On Monday the low temperature at the South Pole dropped 9°F from Sunday's low. On Tuesday it fell another 7°, then rose 13° on Wednesday and 17° more on Thursday. Friday it dropped 8° to −50°F. What was Sunday's low temperature?

   _____

5. Each problem lists the operations performed on n to produce the given result. Find n.
   a. Multiply by 3, add 4, divide by 5, subtract 6; result, −1.

      $n =$ _____

   b. Add 2, divide by 3, subtract 4, multiply by 5; result, 35.

      $n =$ _____

   c. Multiply by 2, add 7, divide by 17; result, 1.

      $n =$ _____

   d. Divide by 3, add 9, multiply by 2, subtract 12; result, 4.

      $n =$ _____

   e. Subtract 2, divide by 5, add 7, multiply by 3; result, 30.

      $n =$ _____

Practice 5-7 Solving Equations by Adding or Subtracting Fractions

Solve each equation.

1. $m - \left(-\frac{7}{10}\right) = -1\frac{1}{5}$ _____

2. $k - \frac{3}{4} = \frac{2}{5}$ _____

3. $x - \frac{5}{6} = \frac{1}{10}$ _____

4. $t - \left(-3\frac{1}{6}\right) = 7\frac{2}{3}$ _____

5. $x + \frac{5}{8} = \frac{7}{8}$ _____

6. $k + \frac{4}{5} = 1\frac{3}{5}$ _____

7. $4 = \frac{4}{9} + y$ _____

8. $h + \left(-\frac{5}{8}\right) = -\frac{5}{12}$ _____

9. $n + \frac{2}{3} = \frac{1}{9}$ _____

10. $e - \frac{11}{16} = -\frac{7}{8}$ _____

11. $w - 14\frac{1}{12} = -2\frac{3}{4}$ _____

12. $v + \left(-4\frac{5}{6}\right) = 2\frac{1}{3}$ _____

13. $a - 9\frac{1}{6} = -3\frac{19}{24}$ _____

14. $f + \left|-3\frac{11}{12}\right| = 18$ _____

15. $z + \left(-3\frac{2}{5}\right) = -4\frac{1}{10}$ _____

16. $x - \frac{7}{15} = \frac{7}{60}$ _____

17. $h - \left(-6\frac{1}{2}\right) = 14\frac{1}{4}$ _____

18. $p - 5\frac{3}{8} = -\frac{11}{24}$ _____

Solve each equation using mental math.

19. $x + \frac{3}{7} = \frac{5}{7}$ _____

20. $k - \frac{8}{9} = -\frac{1}{9}$ _____

21. $a + \frac{1}{9} = \frac{3}{9}$ _____

22. $g - \frac{4}{5} = -\frac{2}{5}$ _____

Write an equation to solve each problem.

23. Pete's papaya tree grew $3\frac{7}{12}$ ft during the year. If its height at the end of the year was $21\frac{1}{6}$ ft, what was its height at the beginning of the year?

_____

24. Lee is $1\frac{3}{4}$ ft taller than Jay. If Lee is $6\frac{1}{4}$ ft tall, how tall is Jay?

_____

Practice 5-8 *Solving Equations by Multiplying Fractions*

Solve each equation.

1. $\frac{3}{4}x = \frac{9}{16}$ _____

2. $-\frac{1}{3}p = \frac{1}{4}$ _____

3. $\frac{-3}{8}k = \frac{1}{2}$ _____

4. $\frac{1}{8}h = \frac{1}{10}$ _____

5. $2\frac{2}{3}e = \frac{1}{18}$ _____

6. $-1\frac{2}{7}m = 6$ _____

7. $-\frac{1}{4}p = \frac{1}{18}$ _____

8. $\frac{11}{-12}w = -1$ _____

9. $-3\frac{4}{7}x = 0$ _____

10. $\frac{2}{3}m = 2\frac{2}{9}$ _____

11. $5c = \frac{2}{3}$ _____

12. $-8k = \frac{4}{5}$ _____

13. $\frac{4}{7}y = 4$ _____

14. $2\frac{1}{4}f = \frac{6}{5}$ _____

15. $\frac{10}{11}n = \frac{2}{11}$ _____

16. $\frac{7}{8}c = \frac{7}{6}$ _____

Solve each equation using mental math.

17. $7d = 42$ _____

18. $\frac{1}{4}y = 5$ _____

19. $-3h = \frac{3}{8}$ _____

20. $\frac{1}{5}k = -\frac{1}{3}$ _____

Write an equation to solve each problem.

21. It takes Nancy $1\frac{2}{3}$ min to read 1 page in her social studies book. It took her $22\frac{1}{2}$ min to complete her reading assignment. How long was the assignment? Let m represent the number of pages she read.

_____

22. It takes Gary three hours to drive to Boston. If the trip is 156 miles, what is Gary's average number of miles per hour? Let x represent the miles per hour.

_____

Practice 5-9 *Powers of Products and Quotients*

Simplify each expression.

1. $\left(\frac{5}{6}\right)^2$ _____

2. $\left(-\frac{4}{9}\right)^2$ _____

3. $\left(\frac{x^2}{5}\right)^3$ _____

4. $(2x)^3$ _____

5. $(-3y^2)^2$ _____

6. $(5ab^2)^3$ _____

7. $(12mn)^2$ _____

8. $(-10xy^3)^3$ _____

9. $(9qrs^4)^3$ _____

10. $\left(\frac{2x}{9y}\right)^2$ _____

11. $-(a^2b^2)^3$ _____

12. $(2a^3b^2)^4$ _____

13. $\left(\frac{2x}{y}\right)^2$ _____

14. $\left(-\frac{3x}{8y}\right)^2$ _____

15. $\left(\frac{3y^2}{x}\right)^3$ _____

16. $\left(\frac{2x^2y^3}{xy^3}\right)^5$ _____

Evaluate for $a = 2$, $b = -1$, and $c = \frac{1}{3}$.

17. $(a^2)^3$ _____

18. $2b^3$ _____

19. $(-9c^2)^3$ _____

20. $(a^2b)^2$ _____

21. $(ac)^2$ _____

22. $(b^3)^7$ _____

Complete each equation.

23. $(3b^{\text{————}})^2 = 9b^{10}$

24. $(m^2n)^{\text{————}} = m^8n^4$

25. $(xy^{\text{————}})^2 = x^2y^6$

26. $\left(\frac{3s^2t}{r}\right)^{\text{————}} = \frac{9s^4t^2}{r^2}$

27. Write an expression for the area of a square with a side of length $4a^2$. Simplify your expression.

_____

28. Write an expression for the volume of a cube with a side of length $3z^5$. Simplify your expression.

_____

Practice 6-1 *Ratios and Unit Rates*

Find each unit rate.

1. 78 mi on 3 gal _____

2. $52.50 in 7 h _____

3. 416 mi in 8 h _____

4. 9 bull's eyes in 117 throws _____

Write each ratio as a fraction in simplest form.

	Boys	**Girls**
7th Grade	26	34
8th Grade	30	22

5. 7th-grade boys to 8th-grade boys _____

6. 7th-grade girls to 7th-grade boys _____

7. 7th graders to 8th graders _____

8. boys to girls _____

9. girls to all students _____

Write three different ratios for each model.

10. ☐☐☐
    ○○○○

11. ●●●
    ○○

12. ▨▨☐

_____   _____   _____

Write each ratio as a fraction is simplest form.

13. 7 : 12 _____

14. 3 is to 6 _____

15. 10 : 45 _____

16. 32 out of 40 _____

17. 36 is to 60 _____

18. 13 out of 14 _____

19. 9 out of 21 _____

20. 45 : 63 _____

21. 24 is to 18 _____

22. 15 out of 60 _____

Practice 6-2 Proportions

Write a proportion for each phrase. Then solve. When necessary, round to the nearest hundredth.

1. 420 ft^2 painted in 36 min; f ft^2 painted in 30 min

   _____

2. 75 points scored in 6 games; p points scored in 4 games

   _____

3. 6 apples for $1.00; 15 apples for d dollars

   _____

Tell whether each pair of ratios forms a proportion.

4. $\frac{3}{4}$ and $\frac{9}{12}$ _____

5. $\frac{25}{40}$ and $\frac{5}{8}$ _____

6. $\frac{8}{12}$ and $\frac{14}{21}$ _____

7. $\frac{13}{15}$ and $\frac{4}{5}$ _____

8. $\frac{4}{5}$ and $\frac{5}{6}$ _____

9. $\frac{49}{21}$ and $\frac{28}{12}$ _____

Solve each proportion. Where necessary, round to the nearest tenth.

10. $\frac{3}{5} = \frac{15}{x}$ _____

11. $\frac{15}{30} = \frac{n}{34}$ _____

12. $\frac{h}{36} = \frac{21}{27}$ _____

13. $\frac{11}{6} = \frac{f}{60}$ _____

14. $\frac{26}{15} = \frac{130}{m}$ _____

15. $\frac{36}{j} = \frac{7}{20}$ _____

16. $\frac{r}{23} = \frac{17}{34}$ _____

17. $\frac{77}{93} = \frac{x}{24}$ _____

18. At Discount Copy, 12 copies cost $0.66. Melissa needs 56 copies. How much should they cost?

   _____

19. You estimate that you can do 12 math problems in 45 min. How long should it take you to do 20 math problems?

   _____

Practice 6-3 Similar Figures and Scale Drawings

The scale of a map is $\frac{1}{2}$ in. : 8 mi. Find the actual distance for each map distance.

1. 2 in.

_____

2. 5 in.

_____

3. $3\frac{1}{2}$ in.

_____

4. 10 in.

_____

5. 8 in.

_____

6. $7\frac{1}{4}$ in.

_____

Each pair of figures is similar. Find the missing length. Round to the nearest tenth where necessary.

7.

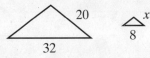

$x =$ _____

8.

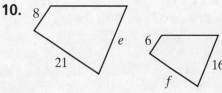

$p =$ _____

9.

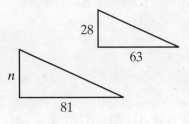

$n =$ _____

10.

$e \approx$ _____ $f =$ _____

11. A meter stick casts a shadow 1.4 m long at the same time a flagpole casts a shadow 7.7 m long. The triangle formed by the meterstick and its shadow is similar to the triangle formed by the flagpole and its shadow. How tall is the flagpole?

_____

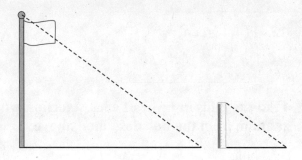

A scale drawing has a scale of $\frac{1}{4}$ in. : 6 ft. Find the length on the drawing for each actual length.

12. 18 ft

_____

13. 66 ft

_____

14. 204 ft

_____

Practice 6-4 Probability

Find each probability for choosing a letter at random from the word PROBABILITY.

1. P(B) _____

2. P(P) _____

3. P(A or I) _____

4. P(not P) _____

A child is chosen at random from the Erb and Smith families. Find the odds in favor of each of the following being chosen.

5. a girl

_____

6. an Erb

_____

	Erb family	Smith family
Girls	2	5
Boys	4	3

7. an Erb girl

_____

8. a Smith girl

_____

9. not a Smith boy

_____

10. a Smith

_____

A box contains 7 red, 14 yellow, 21 green, 42 blue, and 84 purple marbles. A marble is drawn at random from the box. Find each probability.

11. P(red)

_____

12. P(yellow)

_____

13. P(green or blue)

_____

14. P(purple, yellow, or red)

_____

15. P(not green)

_____

16. P(not purple, yellow, or red)

_____

Find the odds in favor of each selection when a marble is chosen at random from the box described above.

17. blue _____

18. purple _____

19. not red _____

20. not green or blue _____

21. yellow _____

22. not purple or yellow _____

■ *Practice 6-5* *Fractions, Decimals, and Percents*

Write each decimal or fraction as a percent. Round to the nearest tenth of a percent where necessary.

1. 0.16 _____ **2.** 0.72 _____

3. $\frac{24}{25}$ _____ **4.** $\frac{31}{40}$ _____

5. $\frac{111}{200}$ _____ **6.** $\frac{403}{1,000}$ _____

7. 3.04 _____ **8.** 5.009 _____

9. 0.0004 _____ **10.** $\frac{40}{13}$ _____

11. $\frac{4}{7}$ _____ **12.** $\frac{57}{99}$ _____

Write each percent as a decimal.

13. 8% _____ **14.** 12.4% _____

15. 145% _____ **16.** 0.07% _____

17. $7\frac{1}{2}$% _____ **18.** $15\frac{1}{4}$% _____

Write each percent as a fraction or mixed number in simplest form.

19. 60% _____ **20.** 5% _____

21. 35% _____ **22.** 32% _____

23. 140% _____ **24.** 0.8% _____

Use >, <, or = to complete each statement.

25. 0.7 ☐ 7% **26.** 80% ☐ $\frac{4}{5}$ **27.** $\frac{1}{3}$ ☐ 33%

28. In the United States in 1990, about one person in twenty was 75 years old or older. Write this fraction as a percent.

_____

■ Practice 6-6 Proportions and Percents

Write a proportion. Then solve. Where necessary, round to the nearest tenth or tenth of a percent.

1. $62\frac{1}{2}$% of t is 35. What is t? _____

2. 38% of n is 33.44. What is n? _____

3. 120% of y is 42. What is y? _____

4. 300% of m is 600. What is m? _____

5. 1.5% of h is 12. What is h? _____

6. What percent of 40 is 12? _____

7. What percent of 48 is 18? _____

8. What percent is 54 of 60? _____

9. What percent is 39 of 50? _____

10. Find 80% of 25. _____

11. Find 150% of 74. _____

12. Find 44% of 375. _____

13. Find 65% of 180. _____

14. The Eagles won 70% of the 40 games that they played. How many games did they win?

_____

15. Thirty-five of 40 students surveyed said that they favored recycling. What percent of those surveyed favored recycling?

_____

16. Candidate Carson received 2,310 votes, 55% of the total. How many total votes were cast?

_____

Practice 6-7 *Percents and Equations*

Write and solve an equation. Where necessary, round to the nearest tenth or tenth of a percent.

1. What percent of 25 is 17? _____

2. What percent is 10 of 8? _____

3. What percent is 63 of 84? _____

4. What percent is 3 of 600? _____

5. Find 45% of 60. _____

6. Find 325% of 52. _____

7. Find $66\frac{2}{3}$% of 87. _____

8. Find 1% of 3,620. _____

9. $62\frac{1}{2}$% of x is 5. What is x? _____

10. 300% of k is 42. What is k? _____

11. $33\frac{1}{3}$% of p is 19. What is p? _____

12. 70% of c is 49. What is c? _____

13. 15% of n is 1,050. What is n? _____

14. 38% of y is 494. What is y? _____

15. A camera regularly priced at $295 was placed on sale at $236. What percent of the regular price was the sale price?

   _____

16. Nine hundred thirty-six students, 65% of the entire student body, attended the football game. Find the size of the student body.

   _____

▬▬ Practice 6-8 *Percent of Change*

Find each percent of change. Round to the nearest tenth of a percent. Tell whether the change is an increase or a decrease.

1. 24 to 21 _____

2. 64 to 80 _____

3. 100 to 113 _____

4. 50 to 41 _____

5. 63 to 105 _____

6. 42 to 168 _____

7. 80 to 24 _____

8. 200 to 158 _____

9. 56 to 71 _____

10. 127 to 84 _____

11. 20 to 24 _____

12. 44 to 22 _____

13. 16 to 12 _____

14. 10 to 100 _____

15. 20 to 40 _____

16. 10 to 50 _____

17. 12 to 16 _____

18. 80 to 100 _____

19. 69 to 117 _____

20. 19 to 9 _____

21. 95 to 145 _____

22. 88 to 26 _____

23. Mark weighed 110 pounds last year. He weighs 119 pounds this year. What is the percent of increase in his weight, to the nearest tenth of a percent?

_____

24. Susan had $140 in her savings account last month. She added $20 this month and earned $.50 interest. What is the percent of increase in the amount in her savings account to the nearest tenth of a percent?

_____

25. The population density of California was 151.4 people per square mile in 1980. By 1990 it had increased to 190.8 people per square mile. Find the percent increase to the nearest percent.

_____

Practice 6-9 *Markup and Discount*

Find each sale price. Round to the nearest cent where necessary.

	Regular price	Percent of discount	Sale price
1.	$46	25%	
2.	$35.45	15%	
3.	$174	40%	
4.	$1.40	30%	
5.	$87	50%	
6.	$675	20%	

Find each selling price. Round to the nearest cent where necessary.

	Cost	Percent markup	Selling price
7.	$5.50	75%	
8.	$25	50%	
9.	$170	85%	
10.	$159.99	70%	
11.	$12.65	90%	
12.	$739	20%	

13. A company buys a sweater for $14 and marks it up 90%. It later discounts the sweater 25%.

a. Find the original selling price of the sweater.

_____

b. How much was the discount?

_____

c. Find the sale price after the discount.

_____

d. The company's profit on the sweater can be found by subtracting the final selling price minus the cost. What was the company's profit on the sweater?

_____

e. The profit was what percent of the cost?

_____

■■■Practice 6-10 *Make a Table*

Make a table to solve each problem.

1. A car was worth $12,500 in 1998. It's value depreciates, or decreases, 15% per year. Find its value in 2002.

Year	1998	1999	2000	2001	2002
Car's value	$12,500				

2. Marcus spent $105 on 6 items at a sale. Videotapes were on sale for $15 each and music CD's were on sale for $20 each. How many of each item did Marcus buy?

Number of videotapes	1	2	3	4	5
Number of CD's	5	4	3	2	1
Total cost					

_____

3. Karina likes to mix either apple, orange, or grape juice with either lemon lime soft drink or sparkling water to make a fizz. How many different fizzes can she make?

_____

4. How many ways can you have 25 cents in change?

_____

5. The deer population of a state park has increased 8% a year for the last 4 years. If there are 308 deer in the park this year, find how large the population was 4 years ago by completing the table.

Year		1	2	3	4
Deer population					308

6. How many different sandwiches can you make from 3 types of bread, 2 types of cheese, and 2 types of meat? Assume that only one type of each item is used per sandwich.

_____

7. A bus leaves a station at 8:00 A.M. and averages 30 mi/h. Another bus leaves the same station following the same route two hours after the first and averages 50 mi/h. When will the second bus catch up with the first bus?

_____

Practice 7-1 *Solving Two-step Equations*

Solve each equation.

1. $4x - 17 = 31$ _____

2. $15 = 2m + 3$ _____

3. $\frac{k}{3} + 3 = 8$ _____

4. $7 = 3 + \frac{h}{6}$ _____

5. $9n + 18 = 81$ _____

6. $5 = \frac{y}{3} - 9$ _____

7. $14 = 5k - 31$ _____

8. $\frac{t}{9} - 7 = -5$ _____

9. $\frac{v}{8} - 9 = -13$ _____

10. $25 - 13f = -14$ _____

Solve each equation using mental math.

11. $3p + 5 = 14$ _____

12. $\frac{k}{2} - 5 = 1$ _____

13. $\frac{m}{7} - 3 = 0$ _____

14. $10v - 6 = 24$ _____

15. $8 + \frac{x}{2} = -7$ _____

16. $7 = 6r - 17$ _____

Choose the correct equation. Solve.

17. Tehira has read 110 pages of a 290-page book. She reads 20 pages each day. How many days will it take to finish?

A. $20 + 110p = 290$　　　　　　**B.** $20p + 290 = 110$

C. $110 + 20p = 290$　　　　　　**D.** $290 = 110 - 20p$

_____

Write an equation to describe the situation. Solve.

18. A waitress earned $73 for 6 hours of work. The total included $46 in tips. What was her hourly wage?

_____

_____

19. You used $6\frac{3}{4}$ c of sugar while baking muffins and nutbread for a class party. You used a total of $1\frac{1}{2}$ c of sugar for the muffins. Your nutbread recipe calls for $1\frac{3}{4}$ c of sugar per loaf. How many loaves of nutbread did you make?

_____

_____

Practice 7-2 Solving Multi-step Equations

Solve and check each equation.

1. $\frac{p}{3} - 7 = -2$
_____

2. $2(n - 7) + 3 = 9$
_____

3. $0 = 5(k + 9)$
_____

4. $4h + 7h - 16 = 6$
_____

5. $3(2n - 7) = 9$
_____

6. $-27 = 8x - 5x$
_____

7. $4p + 5 - 7p = -1$
_____

8. $7 - y + 5y = 9$
_____

9. $8e + 3(5 - e) = 10$
_____

10. $-37 = 3x + 11 - 7x$
_____

11. $9 - 3(n - 5) = 30$
_____

12. $\frac{1}{6}(y + 42) - 15 = -3$
_____

Write and solve an equation for each situation.

13. Find three consecutive integers whose sum is 51.
_____
_____

14. Find three consecutive integers whose sum is -15.
_____
_____

15. Find four consecutive integers whose sum is 30.
_____
_____

16. Jack's overtime wage is $3 per hour more than his regular hourly wage. He worked for 5 hours at his regular wage and 4 hours at the overtime wage. He earned $66. Find his regular wage.
_____

Practice 7-3 Multi-step Equations with Fractions and Decimals

Solve and check each equation.

1. $0.7n - 1.5 + 7.3n = 14.5$

_____

2. $18p - 45 = 0$

_____

3. $16.3k + 19.2 + 7.5k = -64.1$

_____

4. $h + 3h + 4h = 100$

_____

5. $40 - 5n = -2$

_____

6. $14 = \frac{2}{3}(9y - 15)$

_____

7. $\frac{2}{3}y - 6 = 2$

_____

8. $1.2m + 7.5m + 2.1 = 63$

_____

9. $\frac{7}{8}h - \frac{5}{8} = 2$

_____

10. $93.96 = 4.7p + 8.7p - 2.6p$

_____

11. $9w - 16.3 = 5.3$

_____

12. $88.1 - 2.3f = 72.46$

_____

13. $-15.3 = -7.5k + 55.2$

_____

14. $26e + 891 = -71$

_____

15. $2.3(x + 1.4) = -9.66$

_____

16. $(x - 17.7) + 19.6 = 27.8$

_____

Write an equation to describe each situation. Solve.

17. Jolene bought three blouses at one price and 2 blouses priced $3 below the others. The total cost was $91.50. Find the prices of the blouses.

_____

18. A car rented for $29 per day plus $.08 per mile. Julia paid $46.12 for a one-day rental. How far did she drive?

_____

By what number would you multiply each equation to clear denominators or decimals? Do not solve.

19. $\frac{1}{3}z + \frac{1}{6} = 5\frac{1}{6}$

_____

20. $3.7 + 2.75k = 27.35$

_____

■ *Practice 7-4* *Write an Equation*

Write an equation. Then solve.

1. Bill purchased 4 pens for $3.32, including $.16 sales tax. Find the cost of 1 pen.

   _____

   _____

2. Arnold had $1.70 in dimes and quarters. He had 3 more dimes than quarters. How many of each coin did he have?

   _____

   _____

3. A baby weighed 3.2 kg at birth. She gained 0.17 kg per week. How old was she when she weighed 5.75 kg?

   _____

   _____

4. In the parking lot at a truck stop there were 6 more cars than 18-wheel trucks. There were 134 wheels in the parking lot. How many cars and trucks were there?

   _____

   _____

5. The product of 6 and 3 more than k is 48.

   _____

   _____

6. A bottle and a cap together cost $1.10. The bottle costs $1 more than the cap. How much does each cost?

   _____

   _____

7. The perimeter of a rectangular garden is 40 ft. The width is 2 ft more than one half the length. Find the length and width.

   _____

   _____

Practice 7-5 *Solving Equations with Variables on Both Sides*

Solve each equation.

1. $3k + 16 = 5k$

_____

2. $5e = 3e + 36$

_____

3. $n + 4n - 22 = 7n$

_____

4. $2(x - 7) = 3x$

_____

5. $8h - 10h = 3h + 25$

_____

6. $7n + 6n - 5 = 4n + 4$

_____

7. $11(p - 3) = 5(p + 3)$

_____

8. $9(m + 2) = -6(m + 7)$

_____

9. $y + 2(y - 5) = 2y + 2$

_____

10. $-9x + 7 = 3x + 19$

_____

11. $k + 9 = 6(k - 11)$

_____

12. $-6(4 - t) = 12t$

_____

13. $2(x + 7) = 5(x - 7)$

_____

14. $5m + 9 = 3(m - 5) + 7$

_____

15. $5x + 7 = 6x$

_____

16. $k + 12 = 3k$

_____

17. $8m = 5m + 12$

_____

18. $3p - 9 = 4p$

_____

Write an equation for each situation. Solve.

19. The difference when 7 less than a number is subtracted from twice the number is 12. What is the number?

_____

_____

20. Four less than three times a number is three more than two times the number. What is the number?

_____

_____

Practice 7-6 Solving Two-step Inequalities

Solve each inequality. Graph the solutions on a number line.

1. $5x + 2 \le 17$ _____

$\xleftarrow{\;\;}$ −5 −4 −3 −2 −1 0 1 2 3 4 5 $\xrightarrow{\;\;}$

2. $7x + 2x \ge 21 - 3$ _____

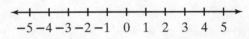

3. $9 - x > 10$ _____

$\xleftarrow{\;\;}$ −5 −4 −3 −2 −1 0 1 2 3 4 5 $\xrightarrow{\;\;}$

4. $19 + 8 \le 6 + 7x$ _____

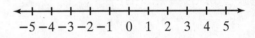

5. $-6x < 12$ _____

$\xleftarrow{\;\;}$ −5 −4 −3 −2 −1 0 1 2 3 4 5 $\xrightarrow{\;\;}$

6. $\frac{x}{-4} > 0$ _____

$\xleftarrow{\;\;}$ −5 −4 −3 −2 −1 0 1 2 3 4 5 $\xrightarrow{\;\;}$

Solve each inequality.

7. $2x - 5 > 1$ _____

8. $9x - 7 \le 38$ _____

9. $3 < \frac{1}{2}x + 1$ _____

10. $-12 < -12x$ _____

11. $-8x + 18 > -22$ _____

12. $50 < 8 - 6x$ _____

13. $\frac{1}{5}x + 6 > -3$ _____

14. $30 \ge -6(5 - x)$ _____

Write an inequality for each situation. Then solve the inequality.

15. Nine more than half the number n is no more than -8. Find n.

_____

_____

16. Judith drove h hours at a rate of 55 mi/hr. She did not reach her goal of driving 385 miles for the day. How long did she drive?

_____

_____

Practice 7-7 *Transforming Formulas*

Use this information to answer 1-4: Shopping City has a 6% sales tax.

1. Solve the formula $c = 1.06p$ for p, where c is the cost of an item at Shopping City, including tax, and p is the selling price.

   _____

2. Clara spent $37.10 on a pair of pants at Shopping City. What was the selling price of the pants?

   _____

3. Manuel spent $10.59 on a basketball at Shopping City. What was the selling price of the ball?

   _____

4. Clara and Manuel's parents spent $165.84 on groceries at Shopping City. How much of that amount was sales tax?

   _____

Transform the formulas.

5. The area of a triangle A can be found with the formula $A = \frac{1}{2}bh$ where b is the length of the base of the triangle and h is the height of the triangle. Solve the formula for h.

   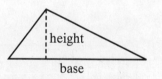

   _____

6. Solve the formula $A = \frac{1}{2}bh$ for b.

   _____

Find the missing part of each triangle.

7. $A = 27$ cm^2

   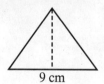

   9 cm

   $h =$ _____

8. $A = 18$ ft^2

   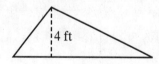

   4 ft

   $b =$ _____

Solve for the variable indicated.

9. $V = \frac{1}{3}lwh$, for w

   _____

10. $\frac{1}{a} + \frac{1}{b} = \frac{1}{c}$, for c

   _____

Practice 7-8 Simple and Compound Interest

Find each balance.

	Principal	Interest rate	Compounded	Time (years)	Balance
1.	$400	7%	annually	3	
2.	$8,000	5%	annually	9	
3.	$1,200	4%	semi-annually	2	
4.	$50,000	6%	semi-annually	6	

Find the simple interest.

5. $900 deposited at an interest rate of 3% for 5 years

_____

6. $1,348 deposited at an interest rate of 2.5% for 18 months

_____

Complete each table. Compound the interest annually.

7. $5,000 at 6% for 4 years.

Principal at beginning of year	Interest	Balance
Year 1: $5,000		
Year 2:		
Year 3:		
Year 4:		

8. $7,200 at 3% for 4 years

Principal at beginning of year	Interest	Balance
Year 1: $7,200		
Year 2:		
Year 3:		
Year 4:		

Practice 8-1 *Relations and Functions*

Graph each relation. Is the relation a function? Explain.

1.

x	y
−1	4
2	3
4	−1
−1	−2

_____

_____

_____

2.

x	y
2	−4
−4	0
−2	3
3	−1

_____

_____

_____

For each relation, list the members of the domain. List the members of the range. Is the relation a function? Explain.

3. $\{(7, -2), (8, -2), (-5, 7), (-9, 1)\}$

Domain: _____   Range: _____

Function? _____

4. $\{(-8, 0), (10, 6), (10, -2), (-5, 7)\}$

Domain: _____   Range: _____

Function? _____

5. $\{(9.2, 4.7), (-3.6, 4.8), (5.2, 4.7)\}$

Domain: _____   Range: _____

Function? _____

6. Is the time is takes you to run a 100-meter race a function of the speed you run? Explain.

_____

Practice 8-2 Equations with Two Variables

Write each equation as a function in "$y = \ldots$" form.

1. $3y = 15x - 12$

$y =$ _____

2. $5x + 10 = 10y$

$y =$ _____

3. $3y - 21 = 12x$

$y =$ _____

4. $5y + 3 = 2y - 3x + 5$

$y =$ _____

5. $-2(x + 3y) = 18$

$y =$ _____

6. $5(x + y) = 20 + 3x$

$y =$ _____

Graph each equation.

7. $y = -0.5x + 4$

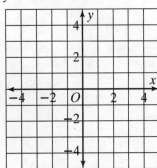

8. $y = 4$

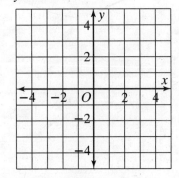

9. $2x - 3y = 6$

$y =$ _____

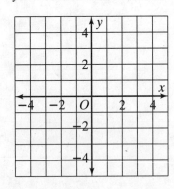

10. $-10x = 5y$

$y =$ _____

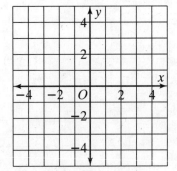

Is each ordered pair a solution of $3x - 2y = 12$? Write *yes* or *no*.

11. $(0, 4)$ _____

12. $(6, 3)$ _____

13. $(4, 0)$ _____

Is each ordered pair a solution of $-2x + 5y = 10$? Write *yes* or *no*.

14. $(-3, 2)$ _____

15. $(-10, -2)$ _____

16. $(5, 4)$ _____

Practice 8-3 *Slope and y-intercept*

Find the slope of the line through each pair of points.

1. $A(1, 1), B(6, 3)$

2. $J(-4, 6), K(-4, 2)$

_____

_____

3. $P(3, -7), Q(-1, -7)$

4. $M(7, 2), N(-1, 3)$

_____

_____

Complete.

Equation	Equation in slope-intercept form	Slope	y-Intercept
5. $5x - y = 6$	_____	_____	_____
6. $7x + 2y = 10$	_____	_____	_____

Find the slope of each line.

7. _____

8. _____

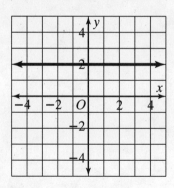

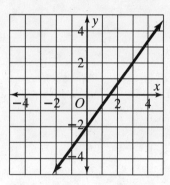

Graph each equation.

9. $y = -2x + 3$

10. $y = \frac{1}{3}x - 1$

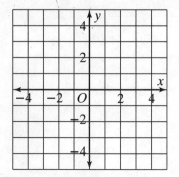

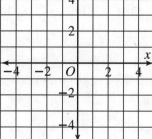

■ *Practice 8-4* *Writing Rules for Linear Functions*

Write a rule for each function.

1. _____

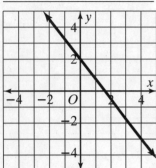

2. _____

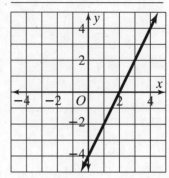

3. _____

x	$f(x)$
-3	18
-1	6
1	-6
3	-18

4. _____

x	$f(x)$
5	-2
7	0
9	2
11	4

5. _____

x	$f(x)$
-3	-17
-1	-11
1	-5
3	1

6. _____

x	$f(x)$
-4	4
0	6
2	7
4	8

Write a function rule to describe each situation.

7. The number of pounds $p(z)$ as a function of the number of ounces z.

_____

8. The selling price $s(c)$ after a 45% markup of an item as a function of the stores' cost c.

_____

9. The total number of miles $m(r)$ covered when you walk 7 miles before lunch, and you walk for 2 hours at r mi/hr after lunch.

_____

Practice 8-5 *Scatter Plots*

Use the data in the table.

1. Make a (year, units of CD's) scatter plot.

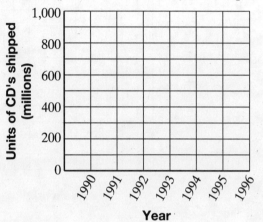

Sales of Recorded Music			
Year	Millions of Units Shipped		
	CD's	Cassettes	LP's
1990	287	442	12
1991	333	360	5
1992	408	366	2
1993	495	340	1
1994	662	345	2
1995	723	273	2
1996	779	225	3

2. Make a (year, units of cassettes) scatter plot.

3. Make a (year, units of LP's) scatter plot.

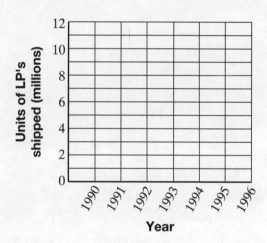

Is there a *positive correlation*, a *negative correlation*, or *no correlation* between the data sets in each scatter plot?

4. (year, units of CD's) scatterplot _____

5. (year, units of cassettes) scatterplot _____

6. (year, units of LP's) scatterplot _____

Practice 8-6 *Solve by Graphing*

A giraffe was 1 ft tall at birth. 7 ft tall at the age of 4, and $11\frac{1}{2}$ ft tall at the age of 7.

1. Use the data to make a (age, height) scatter plot.

2. Draw a trend line.

3. Write an equation for your trend line in slope-intercept form.

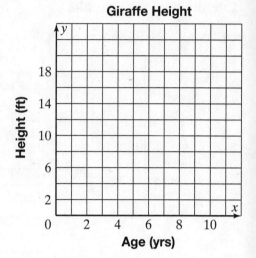
Giraffe Height

_____

4. Use your equation to find the following information.
   a. the giraffe's height at the age of 5

_____

   b. the age at which the giraffe was 16 ft tall

_____

A hippopotamus weighed 700 lb at the age of 1 and 1,900 lb at the age of 3, and 2,500 lb at the age of 4.

5. Use the data to make a (age, weight) scatter plot.

6. Draw a trend line.

7. Write an equation for your trend line.

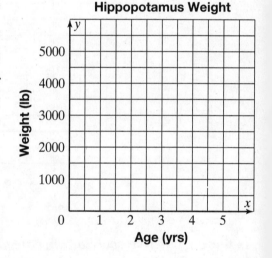
Hippopotamus Weight

_____

8. Use the equation to predict the following information.

   a. the hippo's weight at the age of 8

_____

   b. the age at which the hippo weighed 7,900 lb

_____

9. Can this equation be used to predict the hippo's weight at any age? Explain.

_____

_____

_____

Practice 8-7 Solving Systems of Linear Equations

Is each ordered pair a solution of the given system? Write *yes* or *no*.

1. $y = 6x + 12$
$2x - y = 4$

$(-4, -12)$ _____

2. $y = -3x$
$x = 4y + \frac{1}{2}$

$\left(-\frac{1}{2}, \frac{3}{2}\right)$ _____

3. $x + 2y = 2$
$2x + 5y = 2$

$(6, -2)$ _____

Solve each system by graphing. Check your solution.

4. $x + y = 3$
$x - y = -1$
Solution:

_____

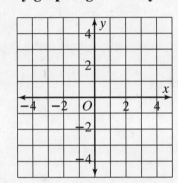

5. $2x + y = 1$
$x - 2y = 3$
Solution:

_____

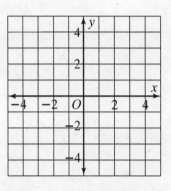

6. $y + 2 = 0$
$2x + y = 0$
Solution:

_____

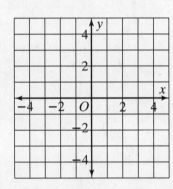

7. $3x + 2y = -6$
$x + 3y = -2$
Solution:

_____

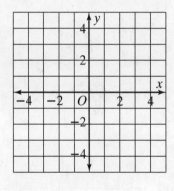

Write a system of linear equations. Solve by graphing.

8. The sum of two numbers is 3. Their difference is 1. Find the numbers.

_____

_____

_____

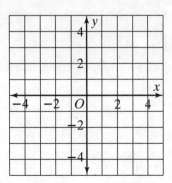

Practice 8-8 Graphing Linear Inequalities

Graph each inequality.

1. $y < x$

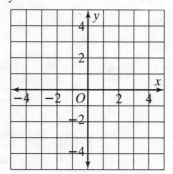

2. $x + y \leq 2$

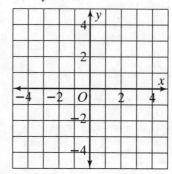

3. $x + 2y \geq 4$

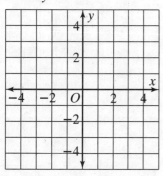

4. $x > -2$

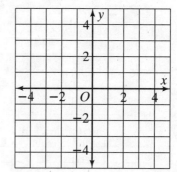

Solve each system by graphing.

5. $y \geq -x - 2$
   $x - 2y < 4$

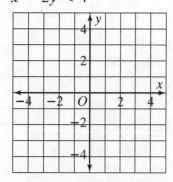

6. $x + y < 3$
   $y \geq 3x - 2$

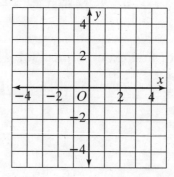

7. Is the origin a solution to the system in Exercise 5? _____

8. Is $(4, 0)$ a solution to the system in Exercise 5? _____

9. Is $(1, 0)$ a solution to the system in Exercise 6? _____

10. Is $(-1, 0)$ a solution to the system in Exercise 6? _____

Practice 9-1 Introduction to Geometry: Points, Lines, and Planes

Use the figures at the right. Name each of the following.

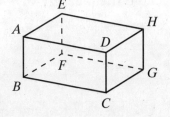

1. Four segments that intersect $\overline{AB}$.

   _____

2. Three segments parallel to $\overline{AB}$.

   _____

3. Four segments skew to $\overline{AB}$.

   _____

Use the figure at the right. Find each of the following.

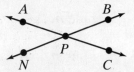

4. all points shown

   _____

5. all segments shown

   _____

6. five different rays

   _____

7. all lines shown

   _____

8. all names for $\overleftrightarrow{NB}$

   _____

Write an equation. Then find the length of each segment.

9.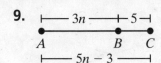

   equation:

   _____

   $n =$ _____

   $AB =$ _____ $AC =$ _____

10.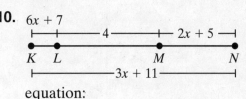

    equation:

    _____

    $x =$ _____

    $MN =$ _____ $KN =$ _____

Practice 9-2 Angle Relationships and Parallel Lines

Find the measure of each angle in the figure at the right.

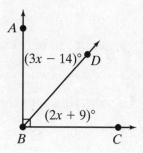

1. $m\angle 1$ _____

2. $m\angle 2$ _____

3. $m\angle 3$ _____

4. $m\angle VWR$ _____

Use the figure at the right for Exercises 5-8.

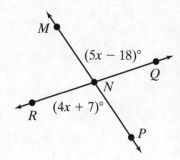

5. Write an equation. _____

6. Find the value of x. _____

7. Find $m\angle ABD$. _____

8. Find $m\angle DBC$. _____

Use the figure at the right for Exercises 9-12.

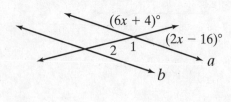

9. Write an equation. _____

10. Find the value of x. _____

11. Find $m\angle MNQ$. _____

12. Find $m\angle MNR$. _____

In each figure, find the measures of $\angle 1$ and $\angle 2$.

13. Given $p \parallel q$

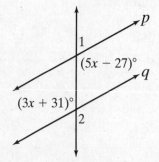

14. Given $p \parallel q$

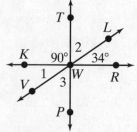

$m\angle 1 =$ _____ $m\angle 2 =$ _____ $m\angle 1 =$ _____ $m\angle 2 =$ _____

15. Find a pair of complementary angles such that the difference of their measures is 12°.

_____

Practice 9-3 *Classifying Polygons*

Name all quadrilaterals that have each of the named properties.

1. four 90° angles

_____

2. opposite sides congruent and parallel

_____

3. at least one pair of parallel sides

_____

_____

Judging by appearances, classify each triangle by its sides and angles.

4.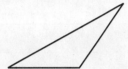

_____

5.

_____

6.

_____

7.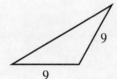

_____

Write a formula to find the perimeter of each figure. Use the formula to find the perimeter.

8. a regular dodecagon (12-gon); one side is 9.25 cm

$P =$ _____ $P =$ _____

9. a rhombus; one side is $1\frac{3}{4}$ yd

$P =$ _____ $P =$ _____

10. a parallelogram; the sides are 10.4 m and 5.6 m

$P =$ _____ $P =$ _____

Practice 9-4 Draw a Diagram

Solve by drawing a diagram.

1. How many diagonals does a quadrilateral have?

   _____

2. Which quadrilaterals always have congruent diagonals?

   _____

3. Find a formula for the number of diagonals d in a polygon with n sides.
   Complete the table to help you. Look for a pattern.

Figure	Number of sides	Number of vertices	Number of diagonals from each vertex	Total number of diagonals
triangle	3			
quadrilateral	4			
pentagon	5			
hexagon	6			
octagon	8			
n-gon	n			

   $d =$ _____

4. One day in the lunch line, Maurice was ahead of Aquia and behind
   Rochelle. Rochelle was ahead of Shequille and behind Whitney.
   Shequille was ahead of Maurice. Who was last?

   _____

5. A mail carrier leaves the post office at 10:00 A.M. and travels 4 miles
   south, then 7 miles east, then 5 miles south, then 10 miles west, and 9
   miles north. At the end of her route, how far and in which direction is
   the mail carrier from the post office?

   _____

Practice 9-5 Congruence

Given that $\triangle GHM \cong \triangle RSA$**, complete the following.**

1. $\overline{GH} \cong$ _____

2. $\overline{AS} \cong$ _____

3. $\angle S \cong$ _____

4. $\angle M \cong$ _____

5. $\overline{AR} \cong$ _____

6. $\angle R \cong$ _____

7. $m\angle A =$ _____

8. $m\angle G =$ _____

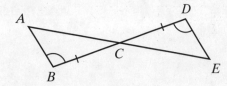

List the congruent corresponding parts of each pair of triangles. Write a congruence statement for the triangles.

9. _____

   _____

   _____

   _____ by _____

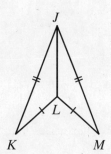

10. _____

    _____

    _____

    _____ by _____

Given that $HPKT \cong BEWL$**; complete the following.**

11. $\overline{PK} \cong$ _____

12. $\angle L \cong$ _____

13. $\angle KPH \cong$ _____

14. $\overline{LB} \cong$ _____

15. $\overline{EB} \cong$ _____

16. $\angle PHT \cong$ _____

17. Explain why the pair of triangles is congruent. Then, find the missing measures.

    _____

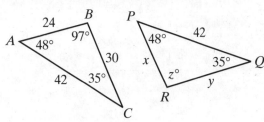

■■■ *Practice 9-6* *Circles*

Find the measures of the central angles that you would draw to represent each percent in a circle graph. Round to the nearest degree.

	Voter Preference for Senator		Central Angle
1.	Peterson	40%	
2.	Washington	30%	
3.	Gomez	15%	
4.	Thomson	10%	
5.	Miller	5%	

6. Draw a circle graph for the data on voter preference.

Voter Preference for Senator

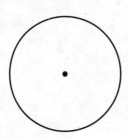

7. The total number of voters surveyed was 5,000. How many voters preferred Gomez?

_____

Find the circumference of each circle with the given radius or diameter. Use 3.14 for π.

8. $d = 25.8$ m

$C =$ _____

9. $r = 9.1$ cm

$C =$ _____

10. $r = 0.28$ km

$C =$ _____

11. $d = 14$ ft

$C =$ _____

12. $d = 5$ in.

$C =$ _____

13. $r = \frac{7}{8}$ in.

$C =$ _____

Practice 9-7 Constructions

Construct each figure using the diagram at the right.

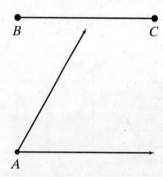

1. $\overline{MP}$ congruent to $\overline{BC}$

M

2. $\overline{JK}$ twice as long as $\overline{BC}$

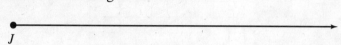

J   A

3. $\angle D$ congruent to $\angle A$ **4.** $\angle PQR$ half the measure of $\angle A$

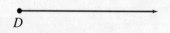

D

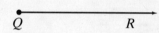

Q   R

5. $\angle STU$ with measure $135°$ **6.** $\overline{EF}$ half as long as $\overline{BC}$

E

U

7. Construct $\triangle WXY$ so that:
$\angle W$ is congruent to $\angle A$, $\overline{WY}$ is congruent
to $\overline{BC}$, $\angle Y$ is half the measure of $\angle A$.

8. What seems to be true about $\angle X$ in $\triangle WXY$
you constructed?

_____

W

Practice 9-8 *Translations*

Write a rule to describe each translation.

1. $(x, y) \rightarrow$ _____

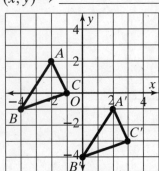

2. $(x, y) \rightarrow$ _____

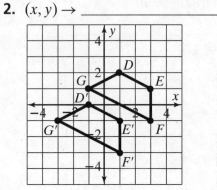

3. $(x, y) \rightarrow$ _____

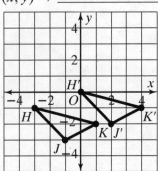

4. $(x, y) \rightarrow$ _____

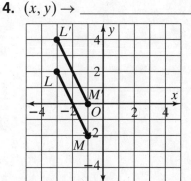

The vertices of a triangle and a translation are given. Graph each triangle and its image.

5. $G(-4, 4), H(-2, 3),$ $J(-3, 0)$; right 5 and down 2

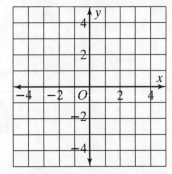

6. $K(0, -1), L(4, 2), M(3, -3)$; left 4 units and up 3 units

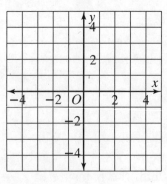

A point and its image after a translation are given. Write a rule to describe the translation.

7. $A(9, -4), A'(2, -1)$ $(x, y) \rightarrow$ _____

8. $B(-3, 5), B'(-5, -3)$ $(x, y) \rightarrow$ _____

Practice 9-9 Symmetry and Reflections

The vertices of a polygon are listed. Graph each polygon and its image after a reflection over the given line. Name the coordinates of the image.

1. $A(1, 3), B(4, 1), C(3, -2),$
$D(2, -4); x = 0$

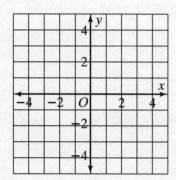

2. $J(-2, 1), K(1, 3), L(4, 2);$
$y = -1$

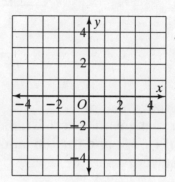

A' _____ B' _____

C' _____ D' _____

J' _____ K' _____

L' _____

Draw all the lines of symmetry for each figure.

3.

4.

5.

Is the dashed line a line of symmetry? Write yes or no.

6. _____

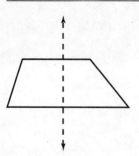

7. _____

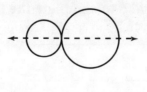

8. _____

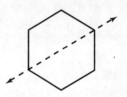

Practice 9-10 Rotations

Judging from appearances, does each figure have rotational symmetry? If yes, what is the angle of rotation?

1. _____   2. _____   3. _____

    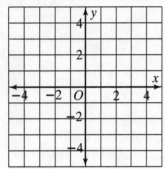   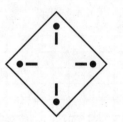

The vertices of a triangle are given. Graph each triangle and its image after a rotation of (a) 90° and (b) 180° about the origin. Name the coordinates of the vertices of the images.

4. $A(1,4), B(1,1), C(4,2)$ 5. $S(2,3), T(-2,4), U(-4,2)$

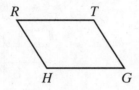   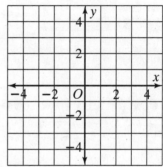

90°   180°   90°   180°

A' _____   A" _____   S' _____   S" _____

B' _____   B" _____   T' _____   T" _____

C' _____   C" _____   U' _____   U" _____

Look for a pattern in Exercises 4 and 5 to complete the following.

6. In a 90° rotation, $(x, y) \rightarrow$ _____

7. In a 180° rotation, $(x, y) \rightarrow$ _____

Name _____ Class _____ Date _____

Practice 10-1 *Area: Parallelograms*

Find the area of each parallelogram.

1.
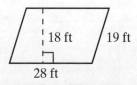
18 ft 19 ft
28 ft

2.
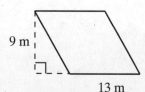
9 m
13 m

3.
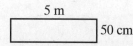
5 m
50 cm

_____ _____ _____

**Find the area of each shaded region. Assume that all angles that appear
to be right angles are right angles.**

4.
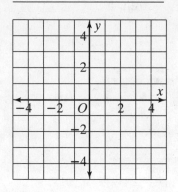
80 ft
50 ft
35 ft
70 ft
25 ft
20 ft

5.
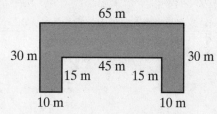
65 m
30 m
30 m
45 m
15 m
15 m
10 m
10 m

_____   _____

**The vertices of a parallelogram are given. Draw each parallelogram. Find
its area.**

6. $P(1, 1), Q(3, 1), R(2, 4), S(4, 4)$

7. $J(-3, 2), K(1, 2), M(-1, -3), L(3, -3)$

_____   _____

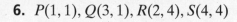

8. The perimeter of a square is 72 in. What is its area?

_____

Practice 10-2 Area: Triangles and Trapezoids

Find the area of each trapezoid.

1.
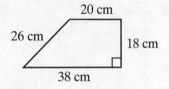

2.
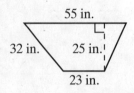

3.
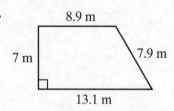

_____

_____

_____

4. base$_1$ = 13 in.
base$_2$ = 8 in.
height = 5 in.

5. base$_1$ = 24.6 cm
base$_2$ = 9.4 cm
height = 15 cm

6. base$_1$ = 2.25 ft
base$_2$ = 4.75 ft
height = 3.5 ft

_____

_____

_____

Find the area of each triangle.

7.
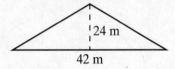

8.
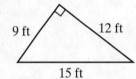

9.
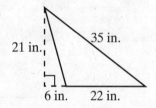

_____

_____

_____

10. base = 24 in.
height = 9 in.

area = _____

11. height = 27 cm
base = 34 cm

area = _____

12. base = 40 ft
height = 8.25 ft

area = _____

Find the area of each shaded region.

13.
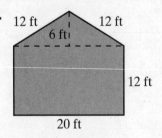

14.
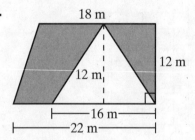

_____

_____

15. A triangle has an area of 36 cm^2 and a base of 6 cm. What is the height of the triangle?

_____

Practice 10-3 *Area: Circle*

Find the area of each circle. Give an exact area and an approximate area to the nearest tenth.

1. $r = 7$ m

A = _____

A ≈ _____

2. $d = 18$ cm

A = _____

A ≈ _____

3. $d = 42$ m

A = _____

A ≈ _____

4. $r = 35$ km

A = _____

A ≈ _____

5. $d = 22$ cm

A = _____

A ≈ _____

6. $r = 25$ ft

A = _____

A ≈ _____

7. $r = 3\frac{1}{2}$ mi

A = _____

A ≈ _____

8. $d = 5$ in.

A = _____

A ≈ _____

9. $d = 9.8$ mm

A = _____

A ≈ _____

Find the area of each shaded region to the nearest tenth.

10.

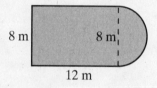

8 m   8 m

12 m

_____

11.

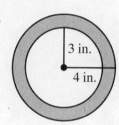

3 in.

4 in.

_____

12.

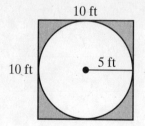

10 ft

10 ft   5 ft

_____

13.

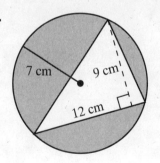

7 cm   9 cm

12 cm

_____

14. A goat is tethered to a stake in the ground with a 5-m rope. The goat can graze to the full length of the rope a full 360° around the stake. How much area does the goat have in which to graze?

_____

Practice 10-4 Space Figures

Name the space figure you can form from each net.

1.
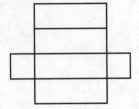

2.

3.
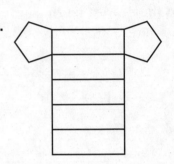

_____   _____   _____

For each figure, describe the base(s) and name the figure.

4.
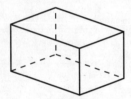

5.
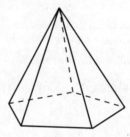

_____

_____

6.
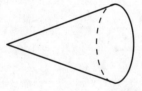

7.
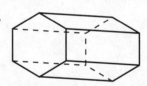

_____   _____

8.
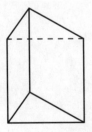

9.
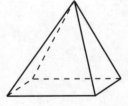

_____   _____

_____   _____

Name _____ Class _____ Date _____

Practice 10-5 *Surface Area: Prisms and Cylinders*

Find the surface area of each space figure. If the answer is not a whole number, round to the nearest tenth.

1.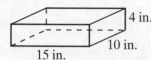
4 in.
10 in.
15 in.

2.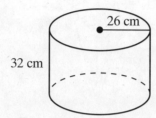
26 cm
32 cm

3.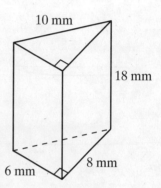
10 mm
18 mm
6 mm
8 mm

_____   _____   _____

Find the surface area of the space figure represented by each net to the nearest square unit.

4.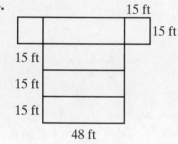
15 ft
15 ft
15 ft
15 ft
15 ft
48 ft

5.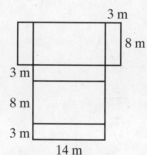
3 m
8 m
3 m
8 m
3 m
14 m

6.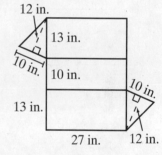
12 in.
13 in.
10 in.
10 in.
13 in.
27 in.   12 in.

_____   _____   _____

7. A room is 18 ft long, 14 ft wide, and 8 ft high.

   a. Find the cost of painting the four walls with two coats of paint costing
   $9.50 per gallon. Each gallon covers 256 ft^2 with one coat.

   _____

   b. Find the cost of carpeting the floor with carpet costing $5/ft^2.

   _____

   c. Find the cost of covering the ceiling with acoustic tile costing $7.50/ft^2.

   _____

   d. Find the total cost of renovating the walls, floor, and ceiling.

   _____

◼️ *Practice 10-6* *Surface Area: Pyramids, Cones, and Spheres*

Find the surface area of each space figure to the nearest square unit.

1.

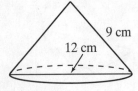

2.

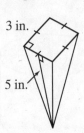

3.

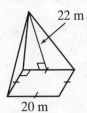

_____   _____   _____

4.

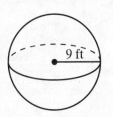

5.

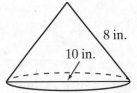

6.

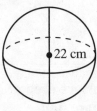

_____   _____   _____

7.

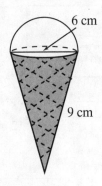

8.

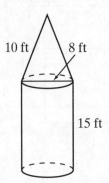

9.

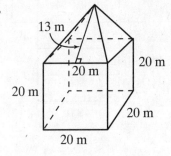

_____   _____   _____

10. A hemisphere with diameter 70 cm

_____

11. A cone and a square-based pyramid have slant heights of 6 in. The
diameter for the cone and the base edge of the pyramid are both 8 in.

   a. Which space figure has the greater surface area?

_____

   b. By how much does the surface area of the greater space figure
exceed that of the smaller? Use 3.14 for π.

_____

Practice 10-7 *Volume: Prisms and Cylinders*

Find the volume of each prism or cylinder to the nearest cubic unit.

1.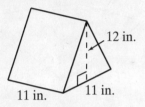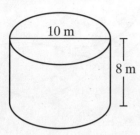

2.

3.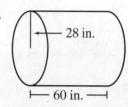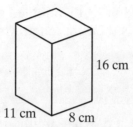

_____

4.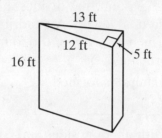

5.

6.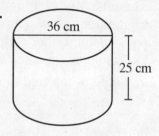

_____

7. prism
rectangular base:
8 in. by 6 in.
height: 7 in.

_____

8. cylinder
radius: 14 in.
height: 18 in.

_____

9. cylinder
radius: 5 cm
height: 11.2 cm

_____

10. prism
square base:
3.5 ft on a side
height: 6 ft

_____

11. cube
sides: 13 m

_____

12. cylinder
diameter: 5 ft
height: 9 ft

_____

13. A water storage tank has a cylindrical shape. The base has a diameter of
18 m and the tank is 32 m high. How much water, to the nearest cubic
unit, can the tank hold?

_____

14. A tent in the shape of a triangular prism has a square base with a side of
8 feet and a height of 6 feet. What is the volume of the tent?

_____

Practice 10-8 Make a Model

Solve by making a model.

1. A narrow strip of paper is twisted once, then joined at the ends with glue or tape. The strip is then cut lengthwise along the dotted line shown.

   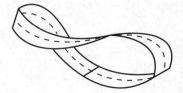

   a. Guess the results.

   _____

   b. Make and cut a model as directed. What are the results?

   _____

2. The midpoint of a segment is the point that divides the segment into two segments of equal length. A quadrilateral with unequal sides is drawn. The midpoints of the four sides are found and connected in order.

   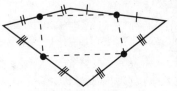

   a. Guess what kind of quadrilateral is formed.

   _____

   b. Draw four quadrilaterals with unequal sides and connect the midpoints of adjacent sides. What kind of quadrilaterals appear to have been formed?

   _____

3. A penny with Lincoln's head upright is rolled along the edge of another penny as shown in the figure.

   a. At the end, do you think Lincoln will be right-side-up or upside-down?

   _____

   b. Conduct an experiment to find out. What are your results?

   _____

4. A net for an octahedron is shown. All the sides are congruent, equilateral triangles. Cut and fold on the dotted lines. Find the surface area of the octahedron.

   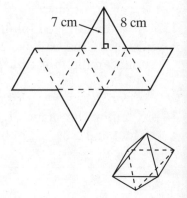

   _____

Practice 10-9 *Volume: Pyramids, Cones, and Spheres*

Find the volume of each figure to the nearest cubic unit.

1.
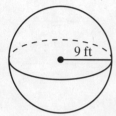

_____

2.
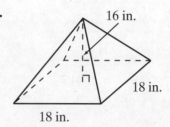
16 in.
18 in.
18 in.

_____

3.
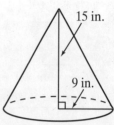
15 in.
9 in.

_____

4.
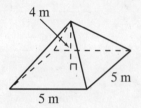
4 m
5 m
5 m

_____

5.
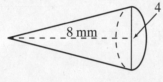
4 mm
8 mm

_____

6.
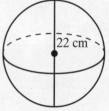
22 cm

_____

7. square-based pyramid
$s = 9$ in.
$h = 12$ in.

_____

8. cone
$r = 8$ cm
$h = 15$ cm

_____

9. sphere
$r = 6$ in.

_____

10. You make a snow figure using three spheres with radii of 12 in., 10 in.,
and 8 in., with the biggest on the bottom and the smallest for the head.
You get snow from a rectangular area that is 6 ft by 7 ft.

  a. Find the volume of snow in your snow figure to the nearest
  hundredth of a cubic inch.

  bottom: _____   middle: _____

  head: _____   total: _____

  b. Find the area in square inches from which you get snow.

  _____

  c. How deep does the snow need to be before you have enough snow to
  make a figure? State your answer to the nearest $\frac{1}{4}$ in.

  _____

■■■ *Practice 11-1* *Square Roots and Irrational Numbers*

Estimate to the nearest integer.

1. $\sqrt{18}$ _____

2. $\sqrt{24}$ _____

3. $\sqrt{50}$ _____

4. $\sqrt{8}$ _____

5. $\sqrt{62}$ _____

6. $\sqrt{78}$ _____

7. $\sqrt{98}$ _____

8. $\sqrt{46}$ _____

9. $\sqrt{38}$ _____

Simplify each square root.

10. $\sqrt{144}$ _____

11. $\sqrt{9 + 16}$ _____

12. $\sqrt{900}$ _____

13. $\sqrt{169}$ _____

14. $-\sqrt{100}$ _____

15. $\sqrt{0.16}$ _____

16. $\sqrt{\frac{16}{81}}$ _____

17. $\sqrt{\frac{4}{25}}$ _____

18. $\sqrt{\frac{121}{144}}$ _____

Identify each number as rational or irrational.

19. $\sqrt{289}$ _____

20. $5.7777\ldots$ _____

21. $\sqrt{41}$ _____

22. $0.62662\ldots$ _____

23. $\sqrt{49}$ _____

24. $\sqrt{52}$ _____

Find two integers that make each equation true.

25. $x^2 = 16$ _____

26. $3m^2 = 147$ _____

Use the formula $d = \sqrt{1.5h}$ to estimate the distance to the horizon d in miles for each viewer's eye height h, in feet.

27. $h = 12$ ft

28. $h = 216$ ft

29. $h = 412$ ft

_____ _____ _____

30. The Moon has a surface area of approximately 14,650,000 mi^2. Estimate its radius to the nearest mile.

_____

Practice 11-2 *The Pythagorean Theorem*

Can you form a right triangle with the three lengths given? Show your work.

1. $20, 21, 29$ _____   **2.** $7, 11, 12$ _____   **3.** $10, 2\sqrt{11}, 12$ _____

4. $28, 45, 53$ _____   **5.** $9, \sqrt{10}, 10$ _____   **6.** $10, 15, 20$ _____

Find each missing length to the nearest tenth of a unit.

7.
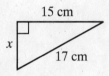
15 cm
x
17 cm

8.
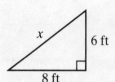
x
6 ft
8 ft

9.
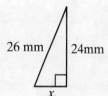
26 mm
24mm
x

_____   _____   _____

10.
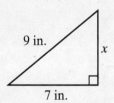
9 in.
x
7 in.

11.
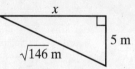
x
5 m
$\sqrt{146}$ m

12.
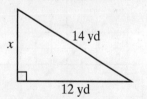
14 yd
x
12 yd

_____   _____   _____

Use the triangle at the right. Find the missing length to the nearest tenth of a unit.

13. $a = 6\,\text{m}, b = 9\,\text{m}$ **14.** $a = 19\,\text{in.}, c = 35\,\text{in.}$

$c \approx$ _____ $b \approx$ _____

15. $b = 24\,\text{cm}, c = 32\,\text{cm}$ **16.** $a = 14\,\text{ft}, c = 41\,\text{ft}$

$a \approx$ _____ $b \approx$ _____

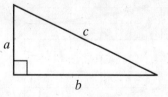
a
c
b

17. A rectangular park measures 300 ft by 400 ft. A sidewalk runs diagonally from one corner to the opposite corner. Find the length of the sidewalk.

_____

Practice 11-3 *Distance and Midpoint Formulas*

The table has sets of endpoints of several segments. Find the distance
between each pair of points and the midpoint of each segment. Round to
the nearest tenth when necessary.

	Endpoints	Distance Between (Length of Segment)	Midpoint
1.	$A(2, 6)$ and $B(4, 10)$		
2.	$C(5, -3)$ and $D(7, 2)$		
3.	$E(0, 12)$ and $F(5, 0)$		
4.	$G(4, 7)$ and $H(-2, -3)$		
5.	$J(-1, 5)$ and $K(2, 1)$		
6.	$L(-3, 8)$ and $M(-7, -1)$		

Find the perimeter of each figure. Round to the nearest tenth when
necessary.

7.

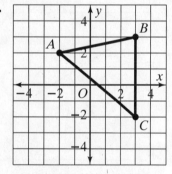

8.

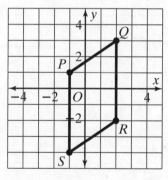

9.

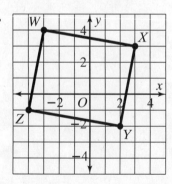

10.

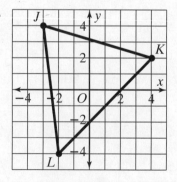

Practice 11-4 Write a Proportion

Write a proportion and find the value of each *x*.

1. $\triangle KLM \sim \triangle NPQ$

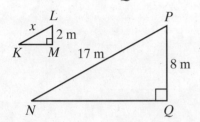

Proportion: _____

x = _____

2. $\triangle RST \sim \triangle RPQ$

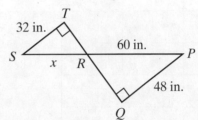

Proportion: _____

x = _____

3. $\triangle ABC \sim \triangle ADE$

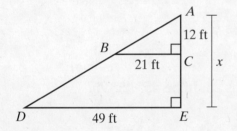

Proportion: _____

x = _____

4. $\triangle UVW \sim \triangle UYZ$

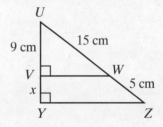

Proportion: _____

x = _____

Solve. Show the proportion you use.

5. A surveyor needs to find the distance across a canyon. She finds a tree on the edge of the canyon and a large rock on the other edge. The surveyor uses stakes to set up the similar right triangles shown. Find the distance across the canyon, *x*.

_____

6. Three cartons of juice cost $4.77. Find the cost of 8 cartons.

_____

7. If a pizza with a diameter of 12 inches costs $10.99, based on area, how much should a 15-inch pizza cost?

_____

◼️ Practice 11-5 *Special Right Triangles*

The length of one side of the triangle is given in each row of the table. Find the missing lengths for that triangle.

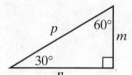
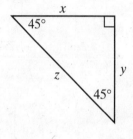

	m	n	p
1.	14		
2.			36
3.		$9\sqrt{3}$	
4.	5		

	x	y	z
5.	11		
6.		8.7	
7.			$7\sqrt{2}$
8.	17		

Tell whether a triangle with sides of the given lengths could be 45°-45°-90° or 30°-60°-90°. Explain.

9. $3\sqrt{2}, 3\sqrt{2}, 6$

_____

_____

10. $10, 24, 26$

_____

_____

In the figure, $BD = 6\sqrt{2}$. Find each value.

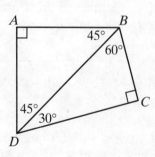

11. *AB* _____   **12.** *AD* _____

13. *BC* _____   **14.** *CD* _____

15. One leg of a 45°-45°-90° right triangle measures 14 cm. Find the exact perimeter.

_____

■ Practice 11-6 *Sine, Cosine, and Tangent Ratios*

Find each value. Round to four decimal places.

1. cos 20° _____

2. tan 64° _____

3. sin 41° _____

4. tan 8° _____

5. sin 88° _____

6. cos 53° _____

Use △MNP for Exercises 7 to 12. Find each ratio.

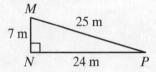

7. sine of ∠P _____

8. cosine of ∠P _____

9. tangent of ∠P _____

10. sine of ∠M _____

11. cosine of ∠M _____

12. tangent of ∠M _____

Use △RST for Exercises 13 to 18. Find each ratio in simplest form.

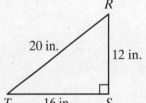

13. sine of ∠T _____

14. cosine of ∠T _____

15. tangent of ∠T _____

16. sine of ∠R _____

17. cosine of ∠R _____

18. tangent of ∠R _____

Write each ratio using square root signs. Use your knowledge of 45°-45°-90° and 30°-60°-90° right triangles.

19. tan 30° _____

20. cos 45° _____

21. sin 60° _____

22. cos 60° _____

23. tan 45° _____

24. sin 30° _____

25. A surveyor standing 2,277 ft from the base of the World Trade Center in New York City measured a 31° angle to the topmost point. To the nearest ft, how tall is the World Trade Center?

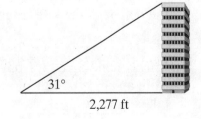

_____

Practice 11-7 Angles of Elevation and Depression

Find *x* to the nearest tenth.

1.

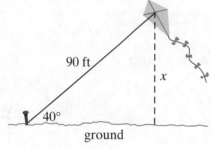

0.75 mi

ground   runway

3°

x

x ≈ _____

2.

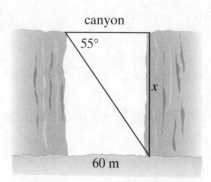

canyon

55°

x

60 m

x ≈ _____

3.

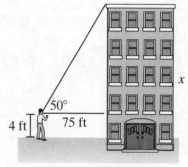

90 ft

40°

x

ground

x ≈ _____

4.

50°

4 ft   75 ft

x

x ≈ _____

Solve each problem. Round to the nearest unit.

5. A helicopter is rescuing a would-be mountain climber. The helicopter is hovering, so there is an angle of depression of 35° from the helicopter to the climber. The bottom of the helicopter's 12-meter ladder is hanging even with the climber. How far does the helicopter need to move horizontally to be directly above the climber?

_____

6. Kara's kite is flying at the end of 35 yards of string. Her end of the string is 1 yard off the ground. The angle of elevation of the kite is 50°. What is the height of the kite from the ground?

_____

7. Karl is standing 80 ft from the base of a tree. He sees the top of the tree from an angle of elevation of 42°. His eye is 4.5 feet off the ground. How tall is the tree?

_____

Practice 12-1 Frequency Tables and Line Plots

Draw a line plot for each frequency table. Find the range.

1.

Number	1	2	3	4	5	6
Frequency	2	0	4	1	2	4

range: _____

```
←—+—+—+—+—+—+—→
  1  2  3  4  5  6
```

2.

Number	1	2	3	4	5	6
Frequency	4	4	0	0	3	2

range: _____

```
←—+—+—+—+—+—+—→
  1  2  3  4  5  6
```

Display each set of data in a line plot.

3. 5 1 4 6 2 6 4 5 1 3 2 6 4 5 4 6

Number	1	2	3	4	5	6
Frequency	2	2	1	4	3	4

4. 4 3 1 2 1 3 3 1 3 2 1

Number	1	2	3	4
Frequency	4	2	4	1

Construct a frequency table from the line plot.

5.

State Average Pupils per Teacher

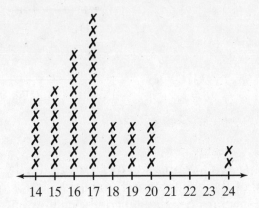

Pupils per Teacher										
Frequency										

6. What is the range in pupil-teacher ratios? _____

Practice 12-2 Box-and-Whisker Plots

Use the box-and-whisker plot to answer each question.

Weekly Mileage Totals, 24 Runners

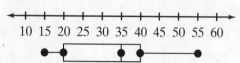

1. What is the highest weekly total? _____ the lowest? _____

2. What is the median weekly total? _____

3. What percent of runners run less than 40 miles a week? _____

4. How many runners run less than 20 miles a week? _____

Make a box-and-whisker plot for each set of data.

5. 16 20 30 15 23 11 15 21 30 29 13 16

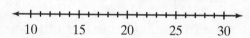

6. 9 12 10 3 2 3 9 11 5 1 10 4 7 12 3 10

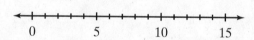

7. 70 77 67 65 79 82 70 68 75 73 69 66
   70 73 89 72

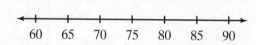

Use box-and-whisker plots to compare data sets. Use a single number line for each comparison.

8. 1st set: 7 12 25 3 1 29 30 7 15 2 5
   10 29 1 10 30 18 8 7 29
   2nd set: 37 17 14 43 27 19 32 1 8 48
   26 16 28 6 25 18

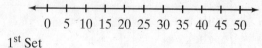
1st Set

2nd Set

9. Area in 1,000 mi^2
   midwestern states:
   45 36 58 97 56 65 87 82 77
   southern states:
   52 59 48 52 42 32 54 43 70 53 66

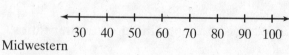
Midwestern
States

Southern
States

Practice 12-3 *Using Graphs to Persuade*

Use the graph at the right for Exercises 1–5.

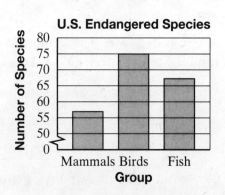

1. Which group of animals appears to have more than twice as many endangered species as mammals?

_____

2. Does one group actually have twice as many endangered species as mammals?

_____

3. What gives the impression that one group has twice as many endangered species as mammals?

_____

4. Redraw the graph without a break.

5. Describe the effect the change in scale has on what the graph suggests.

_____

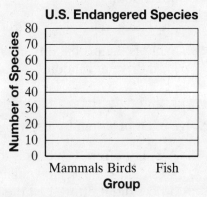

Use the data in the table for Exercises 6–10.

U.S. Union Membership							
Year	1930	1940	1950	1960	1970	1980	1990
Union members (millions)	3	9	14	17	19	20	17

6. Draw a line graph of the data using the grid below.

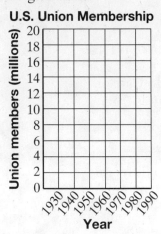

7. Draw a line graph of the data using the grid below.

8. What gives the different impressions in the two graphs?

_____

_____

Practice 12-4 Counting Outcomes and Theoretical Probability

A computer store sells 4 models of computer. (m1, m2, m3, and m4) Each model can be fitted with 3 sizes of hard drive (A, B, and C).

1. Find the sample space.

   _____

   _____

2. What is the probability of choosing a computer with a size C hard drive at random?

   _____

3. What is the probability of choosing a model 2 computer with a size A hard drive at random?

   _____

Solve each problem by drawing a tree diagram.

4. A ballot offered 3 choices for president (A, B, C) and 2 choices for vice president (M, N). How many choices for a combination of the two offices did it offer? List them.

   _____

5. The Cougar baseball team has 4 pitchers (P1, P2, P3, P4) and 2 catchers (C1, C2). How many pitcher-catcher combinations are possible? List them.

   _____

   _____

Solve each problem by using the counting principle.

6. There are 5 roads from Allen to Baker, 7 roads from Baker to Carlson, and 4 roads from Carlson to Dodge. How many different routes from Allen to Dodge by way of Baker and Carlson are possible?

   _____

7. Drapery is sold in 4 different fabrics. Each fabric comes in 13 different patterns. Each pattern is offered in 9 different colors. How many fabric-pattern-color combinations are there?

   _____

Practice 12-5 Independent and Dependent Events

A shelf holds 3 novels, 2 biographies and 1 history book. Two students in turn choose a book at random. What is the probability that the students choose each of the following?

1. both novels _____

2. both biographies _____

3. a history, then a novel _____

4. both history books _____

Meg flipped a penny the given number of times. What is the probability the results were as follows?

5. 2; two heads _____

6. 3; three tails _____

7. 2; a tail, then a head _____

8. 5; five tails _____

Two puppies are chosen at random from a box at the mall. What is the probability of these outcomes?

Free Puppies for Adoption!
5 black retrievers
3 brown hounds
4 black setters

9. both black _____

10. both brown _____

11. a setter, then a hound _____

12. a retriever, then a setter _____

13. both setters _____

Are the events independent or dependent? Explain.

14. A guest at a party takes a sandwich from a tray. A second guest then takes a sandwich.

    _____

    _____

15. Sam flips a coin and gets heads. He flips again and gets tails.

    _____

You can select only two cards from the right. Find the probability of selecting a T and an N for each condition.

M	A	T	H
	I	S	
F	U	N	

16. You replace the first card before drawing the second.

    _____

17. You do not replace the first card before drawing the second.

    _____

■ Practice 12-6 *Permutations and Combinations*

Simplify each expression.

1. $_7P_2$ _____

2. $_7C_2$ _____

3. $_8P_3$ _____

4. $_9P_4$ _____

5. $_3C_2$ _____

6. $_{10}C_4$ _____

7. Art, Becky, Carl, and Denise are lined up to buy tickets.
   a. How many different permutations of the four are possible?

   _____

   b. Suppose Ed was also in line. How many permutations would there be?

   _____

   c. In how many of the permutations of the five is Becky first?

   _____

   d. What is the probability that a permutation of this five chosen at random will have Becky first?

   _____

8. Art, Becky, Carl, Denise, and Ed all want to go to the concert. However, there are only 3 tickets. How many ways can they choose the 3 who get to go to the concert?

   _____

9. A combination lock has 36 numbers on it. How many different 3-number combinations are possible if no number may be repeated?

   _____

Numbers are to be formed using the digits 1, 2, 3, 4, 5, and 6. No digit may be repeated.

10. How many two-digit numbers can be formed? _____

11. How many three-digit numbers can be formed? _____

12. How many four-digit numbers can be formed? _____

13. How many five-digit numbers can be formed? _____

14. How many six-digit numbers can be formed? _____

Practice 12-7 *Experimental Probability*

The table shows the colors of Rahmi's soccer shirts. For each color, find the experimental probability that a random shirt from Rahmi's collection is that color. Write the probability as a percent, to the nearest tenth of a percent.

Color	Number of shirts
red	6
white	4
orange	3
blue	2

1. red _____

2. white _____

3. orange _____

4. blue _____

5. red or blue _____

6. not white _____

7. not orange or red _____

8. green _____

Your school's basketball team has an equal chance of winning or losing the first three games of the season. You simulate the probability by tossing a coin 60 times, letting heads stand for a win and tails stand for a loss. Use the data below. Find each experimental probability as a percent.

HHH THH THT TTH THH
HTH THH THH HTH HHH
THH TTH THH HTT TTT
HTT HHT TTH HTH THH

9. *P*(win all 3) _____

10. *P*(win exactly 2) _____

11. *P*(win exactly 1) _____

12. *P*(win none) _____

13. *P*(win at least 2) _____

14. *P*(win at least 1) _____

15. *P*(win less than 2) _____

Students were surveyed about the number of children living in their household. The table shows the results. Write each experimental probability as a fraction in simplest form.

Number of children	Number of students
0	0
1	11
2	15
3	3
4 or more	4

16. *P*(one child) _____

17. *P*(2 or more children) _____

18. *P*(at least 3 children) _____

■ *Practice 12-8* *Random Samples and Surveys*

A school has 800 students. Two random surveys are conducted to determine students' favorite sport. Use the data in the table to estimate the total number of students who prefer each sport.

		Sport Samples		
Sample	Number Sampled	Favorite sport		
		Basketball	Football	Baseball
A	40	16	14	10
B	50	22	16	12

1. basketball based on Sample A _____

2. basketball based on Sample B _____

3. baseball based on Sample A _____

4. baseball based on Sample B _____

You want to find out if a school bond issue for a new computer center is likely to pass in the next election. State whether each survey plan describes a good sample. Explain your reasoning.

5. You interview people coming out of a computer store in your town.

_____

_____

_____

6. You choose people to interview at random from the city telephone book.

_____

_____

_____

7. You interview every tenth person leaving each voting place in your school district.

_____

_____

Practice 12-9 *Simulate a Problem*

Solve by simulating the problem.

1. Twenty people seated in a circle counted to seven, beginning with the number one. The seventh person dropped out and those remaining counted to seven again. If every seventh person dropped out, what was the number of the last person remaining in the circle? Use the number circle to simulate the problem.

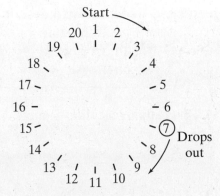

   _____

2. The Rockets played their first volleyball game on Friday, October 18, and played a game every Friday thereafter.
   a. What was the date of their ninth game?

   _____

   b. What was the number of the game they played on February 7?

   _____

3. Five coins are placed side by side as shown. A move consists of sliding two adjacent coins to an open spot without changing the order of the two coins. (The move "2-3 right" is illustrated.) Find three successive moves that will leave the coins in this order: 3-1-5-2-4

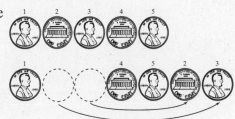

   _____

   _____

4. An irresponsible TV weatherperson forecasts the weather by throwing a number cube and consulting the weather key shown here. The weather during one 5-day stretch is given in the table. What is the probability that the forecaster was right at least 3 days out of 5? Use a number cube to simulate the forecaster's predictions. A successful trial occurs when you roll the correct weather three or more times out of five.

Weather Key
1–clear and warm
2–clear and cool
3–cloudy and cool
4–intermittent showers
5–continual rain
6–snow

Mon	Tue	Wed	Thu	Fri
continual rain	continual rain	clear and cool	cloudy and cool	snow

Work with a partner. Carry out 50 trials. Write the probability after the given number of trials.

a. 10 _____   **b.** 30 _____   **c.** 50 _____

▬▬ *Practice 13-1* *Patterns and Sequences*

Tell whether each sequence is *arithmetic*, *geometric*, or *neither*. Find the next three terms of each sequence. If the sequence is arithmetic or geometric, write a rule to describe the sequence.

1. 7, 14, 28, 56, _____ , _____ , _____ type: _____

    rule: _____

2. 5, 11, 17, 23, _____ , _____ , _____ type: _____

    rule: _____

3. 32, 16, 8, 4, _____ , _____ , _____ type: _____

    rule: _____

4. 25, 21, 17, 13, _____ , _____ , _____ type: _____

    rule: _____

5. 9, 3, −3, −9, _____ , _____ , _____ type: _____

    rule: _____

6. 8, 3, −3, −10, _____ , _____ , _____ type: _____

    rule: _____

7. 2, −6, 18, −54, _____ , _____ , _____ type: _____

    rule: _____

8. 1, 4, 9, 16, _____ , _____ , _____ type: _____

    rule: _____

What is the common difference of each arithmetic sequence?

9. 16, 19, 22, 25, . . . _____   **10.** 3, 5.8, 8.6, 11.4, . . . _____

What is the common ratio of each geometric sequence?

11. 6, 24, 96, 384, . . . _____   **12.** $12, 3, \frac{3}{4}, \frac{3}{16}, \ldots$ _____

Practice 13-2 Graphing Nonlinear Functions

For each function, complete the table for integer values of x from -2 to 2. Then graph each function.

1. $y = |x| - 2$

x	$y = |x| - 2$	(x, y)
-2		
-1		
0		
1		
2		

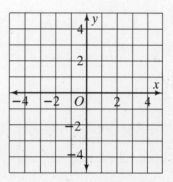

2. $y = -x^2 + 3$

x	$y = -x^2 + 3$	(x, y)
-2		
-1		
0		
1		
2		

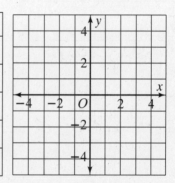

3. $y = 2x^2 - 4$

x	$y = 2x^2 - 4$	(x, y)
-2		
-1		
0		
1		
2		

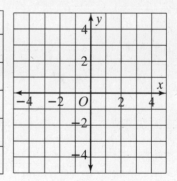

4. $y = 2|x| + 3$

x	$y = -2|x| + 3$	(x, y)
-2		
-1		
0		
1		
2		

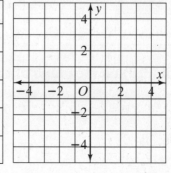

▬ *Practice 13-3* **Exponential Growth and Decay**

Complete the table for integer values of *x* from 0 to 4. Then graph each function.

1. $y = \frac{1}{3} \cdot 3^x$

x	y	(x, y)
0		
1		
2		
3		
4		

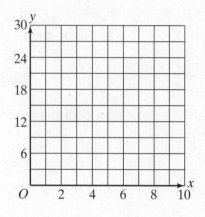

2. $y = \frac{5}{2} \cdot 2^x$

x	y	(x, y)
0		
1		
2		
3		
4		

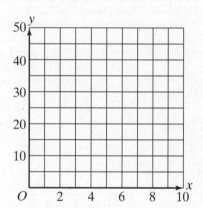

3. $y = 50(0.2)^x$

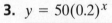

x	y	(x, y)
0		
1		
2		
3		
4		

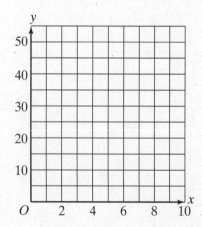

Is the point (3, 9) on the graph of each function?

4. $y = x^2$ _____

5. $y = 3^x$ _____

6. $y = \frac{1}{3} \cdot 3^x$ _____

7. $y = 3 \cdot \left(\frac{1}{3}\right)^x$ _____

8. $y = 3x$ _____

9. $y = x^3$ _____

Practice 13-4 *Polynomials*

Evaluate each polynomial for $x = -1$, $y = 3$, and $z = 2$.

1. $x^2 + z$ _____

2. $3y + x$ _____

3. $2z + y$ _____

4. $x + y + z$ _____

5. $x^2 + y^2$ _____

6. $z - x - y$ _____

Evaluate each polynomial for $m = 21$, $n = -9$, and $p = 28$.

7. $3m - 2p$ _____

8. $2n^2 - 5m$ _____

9. $m^2 - n^2$ _____

10. $n^2 + 5n - 6$ _____

11. $5p^2 - 5p$ _____

12. $7m + 6p$ _____

Solve using the given polynomials.

13. Find the number of diagonals that can be drawn in a polygon with 24 sides.
$N = \frac{1}{2}n^2 - \frac{3}{2}n$
N = number of diagonals
n = number of sides

_____

14. A rock thrown from the top of a cliff at an initial velocity of 3 m/s takes 6.2 s to reach the bottom. To the nearest meter, how tall is the cliff?
$d = 4.9t^2 - vt$
d = distance fallen
t = time falling
v = initial velocity

_____

Tell whether each polynomial is a *monomial*, a *binomial*, or a *trinomial*.

15. $36abc$ _____

16. $10 - h^3$ _____

17. $95xy + y$ _____

18. $a^2 + b^2 + cd$ _____

19. $3k$ _____

20. $-12e + 12f^2$ _____

■ *Practice 13-5* *Adding and Subtracting*
Polynomials

Simplify each sum or difference.

1. $(10m - 4) - (3m - 5)$ _____

2. $(k^2 - 2k + 5) - (k^2 + 5k + 3)$ _____

3. $(2x^2 + 7x - 4) - (x^2 - 4)$ _____

4. $2x^2 + 4 + (3x^2 - 4x - 5)$ _____

5. $(-2x^2 + 4x - 5) + (8x + 5x^2 + 6)$ _____

6. $(3x^2y^2 + 2xy + 5y) - (-2x^2y^2 - 4x + 5y)$ _____

7. $(7x^3 - 5x^2 - 3x + 8) - (10x^3 - 4x^2 + 5x + 9)$ _____

8. $\begin{aligned} 2x^3 - 5x^2 \qquad - 5 \\ + 3x^3 + 7x^2 + 9x \end{aligned}$
_____

9. $\begin{aligned} -4x^2y^2 + 3xy + x^2 - 4y^2 \\ + x^2y^2 - 6xy - x^2 - 5y^2 \end{aligned}$
_____

10. $(x^2 + 2y + 5) - (4x + 4y)$

_____

11. $(-4a^2b + 7ab^2 - 9a - 6b + 13) - (-6a^2b + 8a + 10b - 18)$

_____

Write the perimeter of each figure as a polynomial. Simplify.

12.

5m

$2m^2 - 2$ $2m^2 - 3$

_____

13.

$2n + 3$
$2n - 3$
$3n - 4$ $7n + 2$
$n - 1$
$9n + 5$

_____

Practice 13-6 *Multiplying a Polynomial by a Monomial*

Simplify each product.

1. $4x(3x - 5)$ _____

2. $-8x(x - 7)$ _____

3. $7xy^2(y - 2x + x^2)$ _____

4. $3xy(2xy + 5)$ _____

5. $-9xyz(-2xy + 3yz - 4xz)$ _____

6. $12ab\left(-\frac{1}{2}b + \frac{1}{4}a^3\right)$ _____

7. $-15a^2(a - b + 3c)$ _____

8. $-3x^2a^2(2a^3 + ab - x)$ _____

Write an expression for the area of each shaded region. Simplify.

9.

$12x - 6y$
x

10.
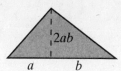
$2ab$
a b

11.
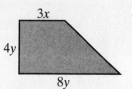
$3x$
$4y$
$8y$

_____   _____   _____

_____   _____   _____

Use the GCF of the terms to write each expression as the product of two factors.

12. $8x + 8y$ _____

13. $13a - 13b$ _____

14. $2x^3 + 2x^2$ _____

15. $11a + 11b + 11c$ _____

16. $x^3y^2 + x^2y^3 + x^4y$ _____

17. $-12ab^2c + 18a^2bc^2 - 30ab^3c^3$ _____

18. $90w^3x + 144w^2$ _____

Practice 13-7 Multiplying Binomials

Simplify each product.

1. $(x + 2)(x + 3)$

_____

2. $(x + 5)(x + 1)$

_____

3. $(x + 4)(x + 5)$

_____

4. $(x + 7)(x + 2)$

_____

5. $(x + 1)(x - 6)$

_____

6. $(x + 8)(x - 3)$

_____

7. $(2x + 5)(x + 3)$

_____

8. $(x - 4)(x - 6)$

_____

9. $(2x - 7)(2x + 7)$

_____

10. $(m - 15)(m - 20)$

_____

11. $(3k + 4)^2$

_____

12. $(x - 20)(x + 20)$

_____

13. $(5n + 4)(4n - 5)$

_____

14. $(10x - 1)^2$

_____

15. $(y - 7)(y - 6)$

_____

16. $(x - 9)(x - 5)$

_____

17. $(x - 10)(x + 3)$

_____

18. $(2x + 3)(3x + 2)$

_____

Find the area of each rectangle.

19.

$x + 5$

$x + 3$

_____

20.

$4n + 7$

$3n + 2$

_____

21.

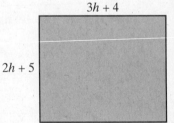

$3h + 4$

$2h + 5$

_____

Practice 13-8 *Use Multiple Strategies*

Use multiple strategies to solve each problem.

1. A rectangle has length $(x - 3)^2$ and width 4. The perimeter of the rectangle is 40. Find the length.

_____

2. A rectangular prism has length $x + 2$, width $x + 1$, height 4, and volume 24. Find the length and the width.

_____

3. A piece of cardboard measures 12 ft by 12 ft. Corners are to be cut from it as shown by the broken lines, and the sides folded up to make a box with an open top. What size corners should be cut from the cardboard to make a box with the greatest possible volume?

_____

4. What size corners should be cut from a piece of cardboard that measures 30 in. by 30 in. to make an open-top box with the greatest possible volume?

_____

5. What is the maximum number of small boxes that can fit inside the large box?

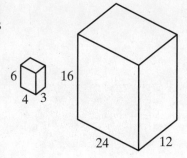

_____

6. The perimeter of a right triangle is 24 in. Find the dimensions of the triangle if the sides are all whole-number lengths.

_____